POLITICS
AND
VOTERS

FOUNDATIONS OF AMERICAN GOVERNMENT AND POLITICAL SCIENCE

Joseph P. Harris, Consulting Editor

Revisions and additions have been made to keep this series up to date and to enlarge its scope, but its purpose remains the same as it was on first publication: To provide a group of relatively short treatises dealing with major aspects of government in modern society. Each volume introduces the reader to a major field of political science through a discussion of important issues, problems, processes, and forces and includes at the same time an account of American political institutions. The author of each work is a distinguished scholar who specializes in and teaches the subjects covered. Together the volumes are well adapted to serving the needs of introductory courses in American government and political science.

Andrew Hacker: The Study of Politics: The Western Tradition and American Origins, 2D ED.

C. Herman Pritchett: The American Constitutional System, 5TH ED.

Hugh A. Bone and Austin Ranney: Politics and Voters, 5TH ED.

Rowland Egger: The President of the United States, 2D ED.

Joseph P. Harris: Congress and the Legislative Process, 2D ED.
  (The two books listed above were revised and enlarged from
  materials contained in the first edition of *The President and Congress*
  by Rowland Egger and Joseph P. Harris.)

Charles R. Adrian: Governing Our Fifty States and Their Communities, 4TH ED.

H. Frank Way, Jr.: Liberty in the Balance: Current Issues in Civil Liberties, 5TH ED.

POLITICS AND VOTERS

Fifth Edition

HUGH A. BONE
University of Washington

AUSTIN RANNEY
American Enterprise Institute

McGRAW-HILL BOOK COMPANY

*New York   St. Louis   San Francisco   Auckland   Bogotá   Hamburg
Johannesburg   London   Madrid   Mexico   Montreal   New Delhi
Panama   Paris   São Paulo   Singapore   Sydney   Tokyo   Toronto*

This book was set in Helvetica Light by
Automated Composition Service, Inc.
The editors were Eric M. Munson and Barry Benjamin;
the production supervisor was Donna Piligra.
The cover was designed by Robin Hessel.
The Murray Printing Company was printer and binder.

Library of Congress Cataloging in Publication Data

Bone, Hugh Alvin, date
    Politics and voters.

    (Foundations of American government and politics)
    Includes index.
    1. Elections—United States.   2.   Voting—United
States.   I.   Ranney, Austin, joint author.   II.   Title.
III.   Series.
JK1976.B6   1981   324.973   80-14899
ISBN 0-07-006492-X

POLITICS AND VOTERS

1 2 3 4 4 5 6 7 8 9 0   MUMU   8 9 8 7 6 5 4 3 2 1

CONTENTS

PREFACE *vii*

1 SETTING AND PSYCHOLOGY OF VOTING *1*

DIMENSIONS OF VOTING BEHAVIOR *1*
LEGAL SETTING FOR VOTING BEHAVIOR *3*
INTERVENING VARIABLES IN VOTING BEHAVIOR *5*
VOTERS' COGNITIVE MAPS *10*

2 SOCIOLOGY OF VOTING *15*

CATEGORIC-GROUP MEMBERSHIPS *16*
SECONDARY-GROUP MEMBERSHIPS *20*
PRIMARY-GROUP MEMBERSHIPS *24*
COMMUNICATIONS PROCESSES *26*

3 POLITICS OF VOTING *31*

PATTERNS OF TURNOUT *31*
PATTERNS OF PREFERENCE *35*
THE AMERICAN VOTER AND THE AMERICAN
  WAY OF GOVERNMENT *40*

4 PARTY POLITICS *46*

THE MAKING OF PUBLIC POLICY *46*
WHAT AND WHERE IS A POLITICAL PARTY? *49*
THE NATIONAL PARTY SYSTEM *49*
PARTY SYSTEMS IN THE STATES *54*
RATIONALE OF THE TWO PARTIES *56*
PARTIES IN THE GOVERNMENT *60*
MINOR PARTIES *64*
POLITICAL LEADERSHIP *65*
NONPARTISAN POLITICS *67*
THE PARTY SYSTEM UNDER STRESS *69*

5 NOMINATIONS AND ELECTIONS *73*

NOMINATIONS IN THE STATES *73*
PRESIDENTIAL NOMINATIONS *77*
CAMPAIGN BEHAVIOR *85*
THE USES OF CAMPAIGNS *95*

6   PRESSURE-GROUP POLITICS   *98*

GROUP POLITICS AND SOCIETY   *98*
THE SOCIOLOGY OF THE PRESSURE SYSTEM   *100*
MAJOR ORGANIZED INTERESTS   *103*
OTHER INTERESTS   *107*
STRUGGLE FOR INFLUENCE: OUTSIDE GOVERNMENT   *109*
STRUGGLE FOR INFLUENCE: IN GOVERNMENT   *113*
PROBLEMS OF PRESSURE GROUPS   *119*

FOR FURTHER READING   *124*

INDEX   *129*

PREFACE

Since the first edition in 1963, many new important works have appeared about American politics and voters. Decisions made by 1968, 1972, and 1976 national conventions, the ensuing campaigns, and the electoral outcomes in numerous states were in several respects departures from their predecessors. These events offer students of politics an opportunity to check their assumptions against actual occurrences. In this edition we have taken cognizance of additional data and of the voting behavior and party stratagems of 1972 and 1976 while retaining the basic organization of the book.

The words "politics" and "government' are simply convenient labels for the way people behave when facing certain problems that have bedeviled them everywhere since the dawn of history. The first part of this book is concerned with the basic unit of all political behavior, the individual human being. It outlines what social scientists have learned about the way people in the United States acquire their political attitudes and about the political actions they take as a consequence of their attitudes.

The second part deals with some of the leading organizations and institutions through which Americans attempt to influence their governments. Particular attention is paid to the composition, organization, and activities of political parties and pressure groups. We note how these groups and ordinary individuals have traditionally brought their political influence to bear: the proposing and electing of candidates for public office. Somewhat greater attention is given in this edition to political participation and influence and to efforts to make political institutions more representative.

Throughout the volume we have tried to present the main facts now known about the way these affairs are ordered in the United States and have offered a number of generalized explanations against their experience and understanding. True learning, after all, is not a monologue inflicted on students by teachers but a dialogue between them from which they gain a better understanding of the bewildering but fascinating world in which they live.

HUGH A. BONE
AUSTIN RANNEY

1 SETTING AND PSYCHOLOGY OF VOTING

Books about politics and government deal mostly with the political behavior of "elites." They tell us about Presidents, congressmen, administrators, judges, diplomats, party politicians, lobbyists, and many others for whom governing and politicking are life's main business. They typically tell us little, however, about the political behavior and influence of ordinary people—people who are only sporadically interested in politics and seldom get nearer the machinery of government than a voting booth.

In recent years, however, political scientists have grown increasingly convinced that in every modern nation, including the more dictatorial regimes, the attitudes and behavior of "the masses" (an unpleasant synonym for "most people") fix the limits within which the governing elite must do their business. In a democratic nation like the United States, periodic elections of executives and legislators (and, in many states, judges) constitute the principal institutional device for making sure that government shall "derive its just powers from the consent of the governed."[1]

Therefore, in the United States among the most critical political decisions are among those determining who will hold public office; for by these decisions we decide who will decide all other questions. That is why understanding American voters is just as necessary for a realistic picture of how our government works as understanding the behavior of the governing elites. Accordingly, the first three chapters of this book will describe and explain the behavior of voters in the United States and assess its impact upon our governing processes.

DIMENSIONS OF VOTING BEHAVIOR

In most studies of voting behavior, and in the discussion to follow in this book, voting behavior is pictured as having the two dimensions represented in Figure 1.

Preference   The horizontal axis in Figure 1 represents the voter's *preference*. It can be used to measure voter approval or disapproval of the

---

[1]For discussions of elections as the basic institutional device of modern democratic government, see W. J. M. Mackenzie, *Free Elections;* Holt, Rinehart and Winston, Inc., New York, 1958, chap. 1; and David Butler, Howard R. Penniman, and Austin Ranney (eds.), *Democracy at the Polls,* American Enterprise Institute for Public Policy Research, Washington, D.C., 1980.

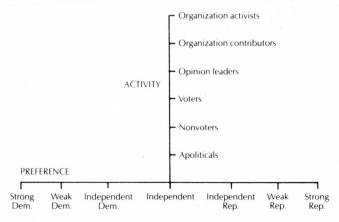

FIGURE 1 Dimensions of voting behavior in the United States.

Democratic and Republican parties, the parties' perceived stands on issues, and the personal qualities of the parties' candidates. The seven main categories of preference are those used by the Center for Political Studies of the University of Michigan.

Activity The vertical axis in Figure 1 represents the voter's *activity*. This dimension has six main categories:

1 Organization activists These are persons who regularly devote much time and energy to working in political parties or pressure groups. They number party leaders and workers from precinct captains to presidential candidates, pressure-group leaders, lobbyists, and the like. It is estimated that only 4 percent of the population belong in this category.[2]

2 Organization contributors These are persons who occasionally make some direct contribution beyond voting to a party or pressure group, e.g., doing volunteer campaign work, donating money, or attending rallies. About 10 percent of the population belong in this category.

3 Opinion leaders About 25 percent of the adult population regularly "talk politics" with their family, friends, and associates and, consciously or unconsciously, influence their opinions and actions. In Chapter 2 the political role of these opinion leaders is examined in detail.

4 Voters The extent of political activity for 30 to 35 percent of the adult population is voting more or less regularly.

5 Nonvoters From 30 to 40 percent of adults vote infrequently or never, even in presidential elections, although most of them still have some trace of interest in political affairs.

6 Apoliticals An estimated 3 to 7 percent of adults are entirely de-

---

[2]The estimates of the proportions of adults in each category of political activity are adapted from Bruce A. Campbell, *The American Electorate,* Holt, Rinehart and Winston, New York, 1979, Table IV.I, p. 211. For a more elaborate typology of activity, see Lester W. Milbrath, *Political Participation,* Rand McNally & Company, Chicago, 1965, chap. 1.

void of knowledge about or interest in political affairs. Politically inert, they constitute the opposite pole of the activity scale from the organization activists.

Understandably, many people concerned about the action of voters in a particular election give most of their attention to calculating preferences. Professional politicians know better. They know that elections are not always won by the candidate "preferred" by the most people, but invariably by the candidate for whom the highest number of votes is actually cast and counted. Thus, if in an election 60 percent of the eligible voters prefer the Democrat and 40 percent prefer the Republican, but only half the Democrats vote and all the Republicans do, the Republican wins a comfortable 4 to 3 victory. Nor is this illustration purely hypothetical, for the fact that there are substantially more Democrats than Republicans in the United States is offset to a considerable degree by the fact that a higher proportion of Republicans than Democrats usually vote.

LEGAL SETTING FOR VOTING BEHAVIOR

Elections in the United States   The Constitution of the United States originally left the regulation of elections and qualification of voters largely to the states, but since the Civil War the national government has played an increasingly important role. The Fourteenth, Fifteenth, Nineteenth, and Twenty-Sixth Amendments limit the states' powers to restrict the franchise. Congress has also passed laws regulating campaign finance and the timing of elections for national offices. Most important of all is the national Voting Rights Act of 1965, in which Congress authorized national officials to put blacks on voting rolls when local officials refuse to do so. Consequently, while it is still true that most of the laws and administrative regulations governing American elections are actions of state and local governments, the national government has increased its role in recent years and seems likely to continue to do so in the future.

The second point to note about United States elections is that in sheer numbers and frequency we are the unrivaled world's champion. In November 1980, for example, all fifty states held elections for President and United States representatives; thirty-four elected United States senators; thirteen elected governors; forty-five elected part or all of their state legislatures; and most also elected hundreds of state, county, municipal, and local district officials. Voters in Illinois faced at least three elections in 1978; in March, they had a primary election for their respective party's precinct or ward committeemen, for district delegates and alternates to its state convention, and for its nominees for the offices of United States senator, United States representative, governor, lieutenant governor, secretary of state, attorney general, comptroller, treasurer, state senator, state representative, county recorder, auditor, county coroner, and state's attorney. In November, they had a general election for all the public offices. Thus, all told they faced a minimum of thirty different contests! In many parts of Illinois, voters also had local primary and general elections for mayor, aldermen, police magistrate, justices of the peace, county supervisors, county assessors, school board members, and so on. This is what political scientists mean by the "long ballot," and American voters have by far the longest in the world.

Thus there is a great deal of voting to be done in the United States. Who is legally permitted to do it?

Legal qualifications for voting[3]   It has been estimated that in the first national election under the new Constitution in 1789 only about one of every thirty adult Americans was legally eligible to vote. All the states excluded women and slaves, many excluded males owning no property and paying no taxes, and some excluded members of certain religious sects. Since then, however, the legal barriers against voting have been razed one by one, resulting in *legal* (though not always actual) universal adult suffrage.

Although the details vary from state to state, the principal legal qualifications for voting today are as follows:

1 United States citizenship

2 Minimum age   Prior to 1972 each state set its own minimum age for voting (twenty-one was the minimum in forty-six states, and the others ranged from eighteen to twenty); but in 1972 the Twenty-Sixth Amendment to the national Constitution set the minimum age at eighteen for all states.

3 Minimum period of residence   Prior to 1971 each state required a person to reside in the state a minimum period of time before becoming eligible to vote (one year in thirty-two states, six months in fifteen, three months in two, and two years in one). However, in the case of *Dunn v. Blumstein* (1972) the Supreme Court declared unconstitutional all requirements of a year or longer. Consequently, at the present time nineteen states require no minimum residence at all, twenty-six require only thirty days, and the others have requirements ranging between ten and fifty days.

4 Registration   Forty-six states have what is known as permanent individual registration. They require would-be voters to apply individually for the inclusion of their names on the roster of eligible voters, and thereafter the basic roster is continued indefinitely and brought up to date from time to time by registering officials. North Dakota has no registration, Ohio and Wisconsin do not require registration of voters in small towns and rural areas. South Carolina requires voters to reregister every ten years, and twenty-one states have recently adopted systems for registration by mail rather than by personal appearance before registering officials.

5 Other requirements   All states deny the vote to inmates of penal institutions and the mentally ill. Some states permanently disfranchise convicted felons, but others restore their voting rights after they have served their sentences.

Generally speaking, these legal requirements closely approximate the democratic ideal of universal adult suffrage. Yet at every election in the United States a large proportion—ranging from 45 percent or so in presi-

---

[3]These are conveniently summarized in *The Book of the States,* 1978-79. The Council of State Governments, Lexington, Ky., 1978, table on p. 235.

dential elections to 90 percent or more in local elections—of the citizens of voting age do not vote. A good many of these, as we shall see later, do not vote simply because they do not think it worth the bother. However, another substantial portion of the nonvoters would like to vote but, for one reason or another, are unable to.

These involuntary nonvoters (we may legitimately call them the disfranchised) have fallen into two main classes. The first has consisted of the blacks in a number of Southern areas who have been illegally but effectively excluded by such devices as intimidation and discriminatory administration of literacy tests. However, the Voting Rights Act of 1965 has effectively put an end to most of this kind of disfranchisement. At the present time, 63 percent of the blacks of voting age are registered voters in the eleven Southern (that is, former Confederate) states, compared with an estimated 12 percent in 1947.

The other class of nonvoters includes those who are ineligible because they are not registered. The Census Bureau estimates that in the 1976 election, 33 percent of the citizens of voting age were not registered.[4] We do not know how many of these people wanted to register but fell afoul of residence or other requirements—or how many could have registered but simply did not try. A thorough study of nonvoting in the 1972 presidential election concluded that registration complications and age and residence requirements lowered voting turnout by about 9 percent.[5] But since 1960 not only has discrimination against black registrants and voters almost ended, but the residence and minimum-age requirements also have been eased greatly for all potential voters. Even so, many analysts believe that only a national law which transfers the main burden for registration from the potential voters to public officials (as is done in most European nations) will produce complete or nearly complete registration of all eligible citizens.

INTERVENING VARIABLES IN VOTING BEHAVIOR

If, in 1976, we had asked some voters why they voted for Carter or Ford, one might have replied, "Because I'm a Democrat"; another, "Because Ford will lick inflation"; yet another, "Because Carter says what he really thinks."

No doubt factors such as socioeconomic status, religion, family influence, and the state of the nation's affairs affect our political attitudes; but our conscious feelings about the parties, issues, and candidates are the most *immediate* determinants of our voting behavior. These attitudes *intervene* between the more general and distant sociological and political forces exerted on voters and their actual votes for Carter or Ford or their decisions not to vote at all. That is why the following three intervening vari-

---

[4]The data on general registration and black registration are taken from the *Statistical Abstract of the United States 1979*, Bureau of the Census, Washington, D.C., 1979, pp. 514, 516.
[5]Steven J. Rosenstone and Raymond E. Wolfinger, "The Effect of Registration Laws on Voter Turnout," *American Political Science Review*, vol. 72, pp. 22-45.

ables are the prime—though not the only—"stuff" of which voting behavior is made.[6]

Party identification One of the oldest and most widespread patterns in American politics is the continuing strong preference of particular regions for one political party. In Vermont, for example, only nine Democrats have won statewide elections since 1854. In Mississippi, only two Republicans have won statewide elections since the 1880s. These and the other one-party systems described in a later chapter stem from the fact that most voters in these areas stay loyal to the same party for generations.

As political scientists use the term, "party identification" denotes a person's psychological attachment to a political party. This can vary in preference and intensity from strong Democratic to strong Republican, and has as its midpoint complete "independence"—the absence of any preference whatever for any party.[7]

No less than 85 percent of the American people express some degree of party preference, although only a quarter confess strong attachment to a party. People acquire their party identifications very early in life; some recent studies of political attitudes in children show that even most third- and fourth-graders say, "We [meaning their families] are Democrats" or "We are Republicans."

In many ways, indeed, the "natural history" of party identifications closely resembles the development of religious identifications. Like most preferences for a particular religious denomination, most preferences for a particular political party are *not* deliberately selected. Rather, most of us "inherit" our politics much as we "inherit" our church preferences; in our earliest formative years we learn about political and religious matters from our parents, and we learn that "our kind of people" are X's rather than Y's or Z's.

As depth of religious fervor varies markedly from one person to another, so too does intensity of party identification. Party politics has its counterparts of the truly devout, the never-miss-a-Sunday-but-forget-it-during-the-week churchgoers, the only-on-Christmas-and-Easter churchgoers, and the people who put a denomination's name on the "religious preference" line of a hospital form but never set foot inside a church.[8]

Finally, we know that changes in intensity of both party and religious

[6] The term "intervening variables" and the analysis used in the text were originated by the Survey Research Center (and later the Center for Political Studies) of the University of Michigan; cf Angus Campbell, Philip E. Converse, Warren E. Miller, and Donald E. Stokes. *The American Voter,* John Wiley & Sons, Inc., New York, 1960. See also the same authors' *Elections and the Political Order,* John Wiley & Sons, Inc., New York, 1966, and the updating of their findings and analysis in Norman H. Nie, Sidney Verba, and John R. Petrocik, *The Changing American Voter,* Harvard University Press, Cambridge, Mass., 1976.

[7] Less than 1 percent of the American people at present identify with any minor party. Accordingly, we shall simplify our discussion here and elsewhere by pretending that the Democrats and Republicans are the only parties around.

[8] Much empirical research has recently been done on the origins and development of political attitudes, including party identification, among citizens of various nations. The leading studies of "political socialization" in America include David Easton and Jack Dennis, *Children in the*

TABLE I Percentage of party identification, 1960–1976

Identification	1960	1964	1968	1972	1976
Strong Democrat	21	27	20	15	15
Weak Democrat	25	25	25	26	25
Independent Democrat	8	9	10	11	12
Independent	8	8	11	13	14
Independent Republican	7	6	9	10	10
Weak Republican	13	13	14	13	14
Strong Republican	14	11	10	10	9
Apolitical	4	1	1	2	1
	100	100	100	100	100

Source: Center for Political Studies, University of Michigan, furnished through the Inter-University Consortium for Political Research.

preferences are far more common than changes in direction. Consequently, party identification is remarkably constant in most people and therefore in most electorates.

Table 1 shows that until recently party identification has been one of the most stable of all forces in American politics. The evidence of history is that large masses of voters switch their loyalties from one party to the other in rare times of great crisis. One such time was the Civil War and Reconstruction era, when the Republicans became the nation's majority party and remained so for more than sixty years. The most recent was the Depression-New Deal decade of the thirties, when the Democrats displaced the Republicans as the majority party and first achieved the dominance that Table 1 shows they still enjoy.

Table 1 also shows, however, that in recent years there has been a sharp decline in the *intensity* of party identifications, especially among Democrats; from 1968 to 1976 the proportion of strong Democrats dropped by a quarter, while the proportion of all shades of independents rose by 13 percent. This decline in Democratic strength certainly did not benefit the Republicans, and it is part of the general decline in popular trust of our political and social institutions characteristic of the era of Vietnam and Watergate.[9]

Party identifications, to be sure, are not the *sole* determinant of people's votes any more than the distribution of party preferences among the electorate is the sole determinant of election results (if it were, the Democrats would never lose a national election). But it is certainly the most powerful

---

Political System, McGraw-Hill Book Company, New York, 1969; Fred I. Greenstein, *Children and Politics,* Yale University Press, New Haven, Conn., 1965; and Robert Hess and Judith Torney, *The Development of Political Attitudes in Children,* Aldine Publishing Company, Chicago, 1967.

[9]This declining trust is documented in Ben J. Wattenberg, *The Real America,* Doubleday & Company, Inc., Garden City, New York, 1974; and Louis Harris, *The Anguish of Change,* W. W. Norton & Company, Inc., New York, 1973.

of the three intervening variables. A number of studies have shown that the most partisan people are the most interested in election campaigns, that they expose themselves to the most political discussion, that they have the most political information, that they have the highest ratio of voters to nonvoters, that they have the fewest defectors to the opposition party's candidates, and that they are the least prone to split their tickets.

The reverse is also true: the least partisan people are the least interested, engage in the least political discussion, know the least about public affairs, and have the lowest ratio of voters to nonvoters.

We have all heard about the "independent voter"—that noble civics-textbook hero who is not contaminated by blind loyalties to any party, who always votes for the best candidate, and who is deeply concerned with public affairs and highly conscientious about doing his or her civic duty. But the 4 percent of the electorate who express no party preference whatever do not fit this inspiring picture at all. They have no party preferences because they have few political preferences of *any* kind; they simply are not much interested in politics and civic affairs. The ideal independent may be a person of proud and free conscience, but the real-life independent is likely to be a person who couldn't care less. In these respects "independent-independents" are very different from people who describe themselves as independents but say they *lean* toward one party or the other. The latter, indeed, are almost as involved and knowledgeable politically as are the strong party identifiers.

Issue orientation This term denotes a person's attitude toward current questions of what government should *do* regardless of what party or individuals hold office. The evidence shows that issue orientation was at a relatively low level during the 1950s and early 1960s. Most people during that period were little concerned with the issues that most agitated the press and the "attentive public"—for example, the Taft-Hartley Act, charges of Communist infiltration of government, and the "missile gap." Moreover, people were more concerned about and had more information on general issues than on specific measures. They felt strongly that economic recessions and the Korean war were bad things, but they had little information or concern about the merits and demerits of specific proposals for economic stability and foreign policy.

Things changed considerably in the late 1960s and 1970s. Studies of the 1976 presidential election showed that most voters had strong opinions on such relatively specific issues as amnesty for draft evaders, government health insurance, busing of schoolchildren, unrestricted abortions, and legalization of marijuana. What is more, most voters perceived Carter and Ford as holding sharply different positions on those issues, and most voted for the candidate whose positions they preferred. There is still some dispute among political scientists about how extensive and permanent issue voting has become in America, but most would agree with the Center for Political Study's conclusion that "apparently it took twelve years of national leadership focused on national problems and policy alternatives to transform the American electorate and to overlay the traditional policies of the 1950s, rooted in the Great Depression and the social cleavages made deep by economic distress, with a new issue politics."[10]

Candidate orientation The term "candidate orientation" denotes a person's attitude toward the personal qualities of the candidates without regard to party labels or issues positions. This attitude has two main components, mixed in various persons in varying proportions. One consists of notions about the candidates' *instrumental* qualities, those which are likely to make them *act* in certain ways. Thus one voter liked Ford because he believed Ford would take a tough line on law and order; another liked Carter because he believed Carter would greatly increase public welfare benefits. The other component consists of notions about a Presidates' *symbolic* qualities, those that make them the kind of persons a President should (or should not) be. Thus, many voters in 1956 "liked Ike" not so much for what he had *done* as President but because they saw him as a man of integrity, kindliness, and aloofness from petty party politics; whereas many voters also expressed dislike of Stevenson because he cracked too many jokes and because he was divorced.[11]

Dwight Eisenhower's immense personal popularity, John Kennedy's Roman Catholicism, the reputations of Barry Goldwater and George McGovern for "extremism," and Jimmy Carter's "born again" religion have given candidate orientation an unusually prominent role in recent presidential politics. The evidence suggests, however, that the impact of the candidates' personal qualities diminishes sharply as the visibility of the office contested declines. It is always important in presidential politics but is probably of very little importance in most elections for, say, county coroner or clerk of the county court.

How the variables interact In every election the question of how people will vote depends upon how their long-run and stable party preferences fit with their short-run and changing views on issues and their opinions of the candidates who happen to be running at the moment.

It should also be noted that if all three intervening variables strongly impel voters in the same partisan direction—if they are strong Democrats, heartily approve large increases in public welfare benefits, and think Carter is a fine man—they are likely to show considerable interest in the campaign and concern about who wins; they are very likely to vote, and almost certain to vote for Carter; indeed, they will very likely vote the straight Democratic ticket.

But what if they are subjected to psychological *cross-pressures?* What if, like many voters in 1976, they are strong Democrats, and feel that Carter is likely to do a better job of maintaining prosperity and full employment but that Ford is a better bet to crack down on crime and check inflation? Such people are likely to have less interest in the campaign and care less about who wins; they are less likely to vote; those who do vote

[10]Arthur H. Miller, Warren E. Miller, Alden S. Raine, and Thad A. Brown, "A Majority Party in Disarray; Policy Polarization in the 1972 Election," *American Political Science Review,* vol. 70, pp. 753-778.
[11]*The American Voter,* pp. 55-59.

will divide their votes more evenly between Carter and Ford, and they are more likely to split their tickets.

A striking example of what happens to cross-pressured voters is furnished by a number of Northern "blue-collar" manual workers in 1968. Ever since the advent of the New Deal in the early 1930s, such persons had been solidly Democratic. But from the early 1960s on, an increasing number came to feel what some call "white backlash"—that is, they grew increasingly hostile to the drive of black Americans for equality in jobs, union membership, residential rights in white neighborhoods, and so on. The Democratic candidate, Hubert Humphrey, was a long-time leading champion of integrationist civil rights legislation; therefore, the candidate more likely to stem the black tide seemed to many to be either Richard Nixon or, even more, George Wallace. A good many Northern working-class Democrats seriously considered deserting Humphrey for Nixon or Wallace, and much of organized labor's campaigning effort was spent on keeping its own people loyal to their traditional Democratic allegiance. When election day came, 31 percent of these workers did not vote at all—a much higher rate of nonvoting than usual for them. A plurality, 32 percent, did vote for Humphrey; but 9 percent voted for Wallace, and no fewer than 26 percent broke over for Nixon—a much greater defection than even Eisenhower could induce in Northern workers.[12]

VOTERS' COGNITIVE MAPS

The voters' feelings about the parties, issues, and candidates are not self-generating. Like other human attitudes, they are formed by interaction between the voters' psychophysical makeups and their physical and social environment. Their behavior cannot be understood by a focus upon only one aspect of this interaction. In most of this book the social and political environment is emphasized, but that *upon* which the environment acts must also be discussed.

The most significant part of the voters' internal makeups is their "cognitive maps" of social and political realtiy. All people carry in their minds a certain picture of what the political world around them is like. This picture usually includes their perceptions that certain things are happening in the world, that these things affect their welfare in certain ways, that what people in public office do in some way affects what is going on and therefore to some extent affects everyone's welfare, and that these officeholders belong to certain political parties, and (in campaigns) that these parties are engaged in a contest in which citizens can take a hand if they wish. Their attitudes toward elections are based upon these interrelationships.

Their cognitive maps also have what psychologists call "affect"; that is, many elements are endowed with favorable and unfavorable emotional connotations. Thus, the voter perceives, say, that at the moment things

[12]These data are provided by the Inter-University Consortium for Political Research. See also Philip E. Converse, Warren E. Miller, Jerrold G. Rusk, and Arthur C. Wolfe, "Continuity and Change in American Politics: Parties and Issues in the 1968 Election," *American Political Science Review*, vol. 63, pp. 1083–1105, 1969.

are "prosperous" (pleasing), but the United States is losing its world leadership (upsetting); the Democrats keep increasing taxes (irritating), but the Republicans care only about the rich man's welfare (angering); Carter's heart is in the right place (appealing), but he is too easily pushed around (not appealing); Ford is experienced (reassuring) but is not smart enough for the job (repelling). And ,so on.

We are all constantly being bombarded by an endless stream of political "signals" from television, newspapers, our families and friends, and all the other "transmitters" in our environment. Not all these signals, however, register on us as light rays register on a photographic plate. Some are received and others are rejected. Those received are sorted among our mental pigeonholes and interpreted in the light of our cognitive maps. To be sure, some of the signals work some alterations in the structure and coloring of the maps, but the typical person's map has a greater effect upon what happens to the signals than the signals have upon the map.

What, then, do the cognitive maps of American voters look like?

Perception A basic principle of modern psychology is that an individual's mental picture of the world rarely if ever corresponds exactly to the "real" world itself. One of the reasons for this imperfect registry is what psychologist Harry Stack Sullivan calls "the mechanism of selective inattention." That is, the external world constantly sends us signals, some of which bring us pleasure and reassurance, and others, pain and anxiety. We do not pay equal attention to all these signals nor do we give them all the same interpretation and importance. Rather we tend to welcome the pleasant signals and give them a prominent place; the unpleasant signals we are rather deaf to, and even if they do force their way in, we try to push them back out of the way where they will not bother us.

We are not saying here that people perceive only what they want to perceive and that everyone lives in a rose-colored world. We are saying that *what* people perceive is affected to some extent by what they *want* to perceive.

This psychological mechanism plays a prominent role in voting behavior, for it tends to distort voters' picture of the parties, issues, and candidates. In the 1948 campaign, for example, Dewey publicly opposed governmental price controls. The Berelson group found that of the Republican party identifiers who also opposed controls, only 14 percent believed that Dewey favored them, and of the Republicans who *favored* controls, 70 percent believed that Dewey favored them.[13] In the same campaign, Truman frequently denounced the Taft-Hartley Act. The Berelson group found that of the Democratic identifiers who also opposed the act, only 10 percent saw Truman as favoring it, and 40 percent of the Democrats who *favored* the act saw Truman as also favoring it.

How can people who favor certain issue positions manage to support candidates who favor opposite positions? In many cases the answer is because they think their man believes what they believe. Like the country

[13] Bernard R. Berelson, Paul F. Lazarsfeld, and William N. McPhee, *Voting,* The University of Chicago Press, Chicago, 1954, pp. 220-222.

lawyer summing up a case to the jury, many of us sometimes reason, "These are the conclusions on which I base my facts!"

Conceptualization   The foregoing suggests that what voters do with the signals after they receive them is at least as important in determining their behavior as the nature of the signals received. Thus, it is necessary to know how they pigeonhole the signals, how they put them together, how they make sense out of what they perceive, in short, how they "conceptualize" political reality.

Levels   Since the 1950s the Center for Political Studies has been asking people what it is they like or dislike about the political parties and their presidential candidates. The thousands of comments have been analyzed for their underlying conceptualizations, and the following four main levels have been found:[14]
   1 Ideology   About one-quarter of the respondents have answered in terms of some kind of general philosophy: they like or dislike one party or candidate because it or he is more "liberal" or "conservative" than the opposition. We shall say more about these labels in a moment.
   2 Group benefits   About one-third of the respondents see politics as mainly a matter of gaining or losing benefits for particular social or economic groups. For example: "The Democrats are for the working man," "The Republicans are the tools of big business," "Any farmer would be a fool to vote for Eisenhower."
   3 Nature of the times   Another one-quarter think about politics mainly in terms of whether conditions are generally good or bad and assign the credit or blame to a party or candidate: "Things have tightened up since the Republicans got in," "When the Democrats are in the cost of living always goes out of sight."
   4 No issue content   Finally, about one-fifth do not mention issues at all and concentrate on the personal qualities of the candidates and somewhat on the qualities of the parties: "Ford isn't too smart," "Carter is a nice guy."

Liberals versus conservatives   From what we see and hear in the newspapers, television, and college classrooms, it seems that American politics is mainly a struggle between adherents of the two great philosophies of "liberalism" and "conservatism." It is not always clear just what the main tenets of these great philosophies are, but we can infer from the talk that "liberals" are for, among other things, vigorous regulation of business, general welfare support of the poor, reducing defense spending, and a conciliatory foreign policy toward the Soviet Union—while "conservatives" are presumably for the opposite on all counts.
   That is how many newspaper columnists, television commentators, and college professors see American politics. Do ordinary Americans see it that way too? Perhaps they do: a series of polls taken since 1968 show that an average of 37 percent call themselves "conservatives," 22 percent "liberals," and 41 percent "middle of the road."

[14]*The American Voter*, pp. 228-248.

But it turns out that these labels do not tell us very much about what *policies* people favor. For example, 71 percent of the self-styled "conservatives" believe that government should guarantee jobs for all, 82 percent believe that government should help pay people's medical costs, and 55 percent even favor restricting the sale of handguns. The self-labeled "liberals" are equally surprising: only 49 percent of them favor stronger government regulation of business, only 44 percent favor increased government spending for domestic programs, and only 45 percent favor reserved job-quotas for minorities.

It is not surprising, therefore, that in its 1978 survey of the polls to see whether or not the American people are, as some have alleged, "turning conservative," *Public Opinion* magazine found that they are turning *both* ways. On the one hand there is a growing feeling that government is too powerful, rising opposition to taxes, increasing support for the tough treatment of criminals, and increasing support for higher defense spending. On the other hand, there is growing support for government health insurance and employment guarantees, increasing support for legalizing marijuana, and increasing support for government wage and price controls.[15]

In short, if the question is, "Are Americans growing more conservative or more liberal?" the answer is, "Yes indeed"—which suggests that the fact that three-fifths of the people call themselves "liberals" or "conservatives" does not tell us very much about the nature of either public opinion or political conflict.

Involvement   The final aspect of voters' cognitive maps is their involvement—the degree of importance they attach to politics in general, and the intensity of their preferences for particular parties, policies, and candidates.

The leading studies agree that a person's political involvement has five constituent parts: (1) belief that a good citizen has a civic duty to vote, (2) interest in following political events, (3) concern that some contestants rather than others win elections, (4) a sense that he or she personally has some real say in how the government is run, and (5) the intensity of party identification. If a person's feelings are strong on all five counts, he or she will vote regularly and perhaps be politically active in others ways. If they are weak on all of them, he or she will be politically inactive in most ways and may not even vote.[16]

As we shall observe in detail in Chapter 3, voting turnout has declined significantly in the United States since the mid-1960s. There are a number of reasons for this decline, but among the most important are changes in some of these components of political involvement. A leading study finds that while most Americans continue to believe as strongly as ever that voting is a citizen's duty and follow presidential campaigns with as much interest as ever, their positions in the other components of involvement have declined noticeably. For example, in 1964, 69 percent of the

[15] *Public Opinion,* September–October 1978, pp. 33–39.
[16] *The American Voter,* chap. 5; and Richard A. Brody and Paul M. Sniderman, "From Life Space to Polling Place," *British Journal of Political Science,* vol. 7, pp. 337–360.

people said that they cared quite a lot about who won the Johnson-Goldwater presidential contest. In 1976, however, only 57 percent said they cared much about whether Carter or Ford won. For another example, in 1960, 75 percent of the people said that they believed that ordinary people have a real say in how the government is run. In 1976, however, only 46 percent said so. And in Table 1 we have already set forth the details on the decline in party identification.[17]

Thus most Americans in the 1980s do not see politics as something that can preserve or destroy their most cherished values, nor does any particular election seem to them to be a great crisis in the continuing struggle between good and evil. For most of them elections can be entertaining spectacles, and it is often interesting to know who is ahead, who is gaining, and who is falling back. But Election Day is rather like Sunday: not a day of reckoning, but a time to do one's civic duty—if, that is, it is not too inconvenient or boring.

Is that attitude good or bad for the health of American democracy? We shall return to this question in Chapter 3, but first we need to look at the sociology and politics of voting as well as the psychology we have examined in this chapter.

REVIEW QUESTIONS

1 Where would you locate yourself on the scales of voting behavior illustrated in Figure 1? What about your parents? Your closest friends?

2 What arguments can you make both for an against denying the vote to poor people? Blacks? Women? Communists? People under twenty-one years of age?

3 What is your present party identification? Has it ever changed? When did you first acquire it? How?

4 What present-day American political leader do you most admire? Why? Which leader do you most dislike? Why? Are you mainly concerned with their "instrumental" or "symbolic" qualities?

5 Describe with illustrations the nature of "psychological cross pressures" on voting. Do you personally know anyone particularly subject to such pressures? If so, how does that person resolve these conflicts?

6 As far as you can tell, what are the most prominent features of your own "cognitive map" of political reality? In what, if any, respects do you think it differs from that of most other people?

7 Do you think it would be good or bad if a great many more Americans become more involved politically than they are now? Why?

[17] Richard A. Brody, "The Puzzle of Political Participation in America," in Anthony King (ed.), *The New American Political System,* American Enterprise Institute for Public Policy Research, Washington, D.C., 1978, pp. 287–324.

2 SOCIOLOGY OF VOTING

No doubt we would all like to believe that we have chosen our religion, our tastes, and our politics deliberately and independently, as free and rational beings. But we must recognize that we have learned most of these things from "significant others"—from our parents, ministers, teachers, spouses, and friends.

We are never entirely "liberated" from social influences and strike out wholly on our own. Sociologists and social psychologists tell us that throughout our lives our attitudes and behavior are profoundly influenced by "reference groups." That is, when confronted with something new—a new style in dress, a black trying to buy a home in our for-whites-only neighborhood, or the latest election—we do not consider the problem entirely in splendid isolation from what all other people are thinking and saying. Rather we become aware of how other people—not all other people, but some other people—are reacting; we "refer" to the views of others. If they all are reacting in the same way, that is probably how we also will react. If their reactions are mixed, we will be caught in cross pressures, with consequences similar to those described in the preceding chapter.

The main reference groups for some of us may be our families, for others labor unions and fraternal societies, for still others churches. Consequently, no social or political event is ever reacted to in exactly the same way by all Americans; *differential* reaction to each event is a basic trait of our society.

And so it is with voting behavior. Chapter 1 showed how people's cognitive maps differ. These differences are not random, and voters do not acquire their views by pure chance. The intervening variables of voting psychology are deeply affected by the structure and processes of American society. Striking evidence for this basic proposition is furnished by Table 2.

In each election year no more than three of the social groups divided exactly as the entire electorate did. Many groups deviated from the national division by more than 10 percentage points. In short, whereas no social group acts unanimously, many have distinct central political tendencies that stem from their position in the society. There are three main types of groups.

1 Categoric groups Each of these consists of people who share one or more characteristics (e.g., high school graduates, men, age group),

TABLE 2 Presidential preferences of social groups, 1960–1972

Social group	Percent favoring Republican				
	1960	*1964*	*1968*	*1972*	*1976*
Entire electorate*	49.5	38.7	43.4	60.7	48.0
Men	48	40	43	63	45
Women	51	38	43	62	51
White	51	41	47	68	52
Nonwhite	32	6	12	13	15
Grade school educated	45	34	33	51	41
High school educated	48	38	43	66	46
College educated	61	48	54	63	55
Age group 21–29	46	36	38	52†	45†
Age group 30–49	46	37	41	67	49
Age group over 50	54	41	47	64	48
Protestants	62	45	49	70	53
Roman Catholics	22	24	33	52	42
Professional and business workers	58	46	56	69	56
White-collar workers	52	43	47	64	48
Manual workers	40	29	35	57	41
Farmers	52	47	51	—	—

*Official returns.
†Age group 18–29.
Source: Gallup Opinion Index, Release of December 1972, p. 10. *The Gallup Poll: Public Opinion, 1972–1977*, Scholarly Resources, Inc., 1978, vol. 2, pp. 909–910.

who do not have conscious group identifications, goals, or organized political activity, but whose political behavior nevertheless has distinctive group characteristics.

2 Secondary groups Each of these consists of people sharing one or more traits (e.g., blacks, medical doctors, Catholics) who to some extent have conscious group identifications and goals, and some of whom form organizations to advance the group's interest (e.g., the National Association for the Advancement of Colored People, the American Medical Association).

3 Primary groups Each of these consists of people who have regular and frequent face-to-face contacts and interactions (e.g., husbands and wives, parents and children, friends, coworkers).

CATEGORIC-GROUP MEMBERSHIPS

Generally speaking, the distinctive political behavior of a categoric group depends on its reaction to a variety of factors. (1) Political events: An increase in governmental old-age benefits, for example, eases the financial worries of people over sixty-five and increases the tax burdens on people under sixty-five. (2) Political experiences: People over sixty-five, for instance, are more aware than people under thirty of problems arising from inflation and the rising costs of medical care. (3) Social roles: It used to be perfectly acceptable, particularly among the less educated, for example, for a woman to say that politics is a man's business and that she votes as her husband tells her to; but it was a brave man indeed who would publicly confess that his wife told him how to vote!

The most significant categoric-group divisions in American politics are the following.

Sex   Women now outnumber men in the United States by a ratio of 51 to 49, but as a somewhat lower proportion of women than men usually vote, the electorate is almost evenly divided between the sexes. There appear to be no significant sexual differences in political preferences, but women's political activity still differs slightly from men's. Women are generally less involved, interested, and active in politics than men. They are less likely than men to feel that their vote "matters" or that they have any civic duty to vote.

The traditional political inactivity of women evidently has resulted mainly from the view once widely held, especially in the lower socioeconomic levels of our society, that a woman's proper business is caring for her home, her husband, and her children, and she should leave the rough and dirty world of business and politics to her menfolk.[1]

These sexual differences have always been much narrower in the higher educational levels, where women have long been taught that they should play a part in civic affairs equal to that of men. They are also narrowing and may eventually disappear altogether among women at all educational levels as part of the changing general ideas about the proper role of women in society.[2]

Age   Current census figures show a steady increase since 1960 in the proportion of our population at both extremes of the age continuum. At present 30 percent of Americans are in the pre-adult category of ages seventeen and under, 59 percent are in the "productive years" of eighteen to sixty-four, and 11 percent are in the post-retirement category of sixty-five and older.

These figures have political significance as well, for there are noteworthy differences in the voting behavior of various age groups. For one thing, there is a slight but distinct tendency for people to grow more conservative and less tolerant of opposing views as they grow older.[3] Much stronger,

[1]Charles E. Merriam and Harold F. Gosnell, *Nonvoting,* The University of Chicago Press, Chicago, 1924, pp. 112–113; and Paul F. Lazarsfeld, Bernard R. Berelson, and Hazel Gaudet, *The People's Choice,* 2d ed., Columbia University Press, New York, 1948, p. 49.

[2]Cf. Jeane J. Kirkpatrick, *Political Woman,* Basic Books, New York, 1974; and Angus Campbell, Philip E. Converse, Warren E. Miller, and Donald E. Stokes, *The American Voter,* John Wiley & Sons, Inc., New York, 1960, pp. 483–493.

[3]Cf. Herbert H. Hyman, *Political Socialization,* The Free Press, New York, 1959, chap. 6.

PERCENT VOTING

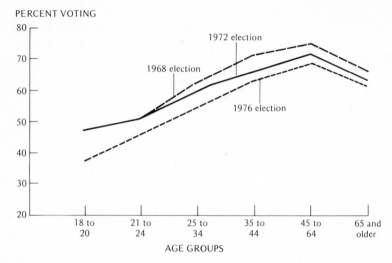

FIGURE 2 Voting turnout by various age groups in 1968, 1972, and 1976. (Data from the Bureau of the Census.)

however, is the tendency for people, as they grow older, to become politically more involved, more partisan, and more active. Activity rates grow steadily higher in each successively older group up to those in their early sixties, when increasing physical infirmities begin to inhibit activity of all kinds. These age differentials, moreover, exist in all educational and social categories: young people in all strata of society are more apathetic about politics than older people. The role of age is illustrated graphically by the age-voting turnout curve shown in Figure 2.

Part of the explanation for the pattern shown in Figure 2 lies in the fact that as most persons age they acquire families, jobs, and property; they pay taxes; they become increasingly aware of the impact of government policies on their welfare; consequently, their personal stakes in politics increase and become more evident. The main motivating factor, however, is that the depth and strength of their party identifications increase. The Center for Political Research has found that the longer people belong to a party, the deeper grows their attachment to it, and their increasing partisanship in turn produces increasing political involvement and greater activity in the manner described in Chapter 1 and illustrated in Figure 2. For as we have seen, a strong party identification provides people with a psychological sorting device for giving some order and meaning to the "booming, buzzing confusion" of the world of politics—a device that many of them would otherwise lack. The older they get the better this partisan "sorter" works, and the more active they become as a result.[4]

Education   Americans grow steadily more educated—at least in terms of the number of school years completed. From 1950 to 1980 the proportion of adults with some college education increased from 8 to 28 percent, those with some high school education increased from 47 to 54 percent, and those with only grade school education declined from 45 to 18 percent.

This too is likely to have political repercussions. The studies of voting behavior show that a high proportion of the most educated people are Republicans and a majority of the least educated are Democrats. We should hesitate, however, to conclude that the informing and enlightening processes of formal education just naturally lead people to Republicanism (or, for that matter, Democracy). For the voting studies also show that most persons high on the social and economic scale are Republicans and that they are also the most educated. Thus, some chicken-or-egg questions of causation arise: Do rich people have the most formal education because they can afford it, or do educated people earn the most money because they are the best trained? In other words, what comes first, the money or the education? By the same token, are the most educated, best-off people Republicans because of education or because they believe the Republicans best protect their preferred economic and social positions?

For the answers to these questions, the Center for Political Studies found that *within* particular occupational and income groups, educational differences make little or no difference in partisanship. In other words, most bankers went to college and are Republicans, whereas most factory workers did not go to college and are Democrats; *but* the few bankers who did not go to college are just as Republican as the bankers who did, and the few factory workers who did go to college are just as Democratic as the workers who did not. Thus it seems that education, considered by itself, has little effect on making people Republicans or Democrats.

A very different situation, however, exists with regard to political *activity*. The best educated are the most active, and the least educated are the least active. The highly educated are also the most interested in politics and the most concerned with election results; they have the smallest proportion of nonvoters and the highest proportion at the upper levels of our activity scale (see Figure 1); and they talk politics more and provide more "opinion leaders" than any other stratum of the population.

Apparently education gives people the psychological apparatus they need for ordering and making sense out of political events. As a result, college people generally find more meaning in politics than the less educated and derive greater satisfaction from active participation.[5] Thus we might expect that as Americans become more educated they will grow politically more active. Yet, despite the fact that their levels of education have continued to rise steadily in recent years. Americans have in fact been voting in steadily *decreasing* proportions. We shall have more to say about this strange turn of events in Chapter 3.

[5]Ibid., pp. 475–481.

SECONDARY-GROUP MEMBERSHIPS

Secondary-group influences on voting behavior are on the whole more powerful than those of categoric groups. Like categoric groups, secondary groups are differentially affected by governmental policies and differentially exposed to political experiences and have different social roles. These factors are reinforced by the conscious group identifications and goals of the members and by the continuing efforts of the particular group's leaders to solidify the members' preferences and to get them to contribute actively to the group's efforts.

Nevertheless, no secondary group ever mobilizes *all* its members behind any party, candidate, or public policy. In every group at any given time some members make the group and its interest the central concern of their lives and are ever ready to rush to the barricades when the trumpet sounds; others see it as merely one of a number of worthy causes deserving attention and only occasionally heed its pleas; still others are scarcely aware of the group's existence or their connection with it and couldn't care less about its calls to duty.

The influence of a secondary group on any one of its members is the product of several psychological factors. The first is the strength of the individual's identification with the group. In general, the more conscious he is of being a Jew or a black or a labor union member, the stronger the group's political influence on him. This, in turn, is related to the length of his membership in the group. The longer the membership, the stronger his psychological involvement with it. The third factor is the salience of politics for the group's leaders. The more important politics seems to them, the more they will insist that particular political actions are marks of group loyalty, and the harder it will be for a group member to act otherwise. The final factor is the importance of politics for the individual member. If he or she holds views deviant from the group's, and if those views are regarded as personally important, he or she will be hard to bring into line; but if politics seems relatively unimportant, or at least less important than the relationship to the group, he or she is more likely to do as they wish.

The differential operation of these factors in individuals means that the political influence of any secondary group varies among its members and that there will also be substantial differences from one group to another in the solidarity of the members' preferences and the degree of their activity.

These group differentials are important data for the analysis of politics. For example, knowing that a majority of Protestants opposed Kennedy and a majority of Catholics favored him in 1960 does not tell us much about the role of religion in that election. We need to know the *proportions* of Protestants against him and Catholics for him and whether either proportion was noticeably greater than the usual proportion of Protestants for Republicans and Catholics for Democrats. We also need to know whether either or both groups were noticeably more active in 1960 than in previous years. Only when we get the answers to these and similar questions can we begin a serious assessment of the role of religion in the 1960 election. Thus it is with the question of secondary-group influences in any election.

The secondary groups generally regarded as most influential in American politics can be classified under the following headings:

Occupation   The 1970 census showed that increasing proportions of the nation's work force are going into the higher-status occupations. According to the occupational categories listed in Table 2, the proportion in the professions increased from 18 to 26 percent between 1950 and 1977, that in the white-collar occupations increased from 20 to 24 percent, that in manual labor decreased from 50 to 47 percent, and farming slipped from 12 to 3 percent. The voting studies have generally found that people in the higher-status occupations tend to be more Republican and more active than those in the lower-status occupations, so that the continuation of these shifts in the distribution of the work force may well have substantial political effects in the 1980s.

Aside from its effect on general social position, a person's occupation can affect his or her political outlook. It determines the kind of people he or she sees every day and thus fixes many of the primary-group influences to which he or she is subject. And these are the most powerful of all social influences on voting behavior. Many occupations, moreover, have specific political goals and organize to mobilize their members for political action. The mere mention of some of the leading groups—the American Medical Association, the United Auto Workers, the American Farm Bureau Federation, the National Education Association—indicates the variety and potency of the highly "politicized" occupational groups in American society.

Socioeconomic status and social class   We Americans have mixed feelings about matters of social status and class. On one hand, many of us find repugnant the whole idea of class distinctions and prefer to cling to our traditional view that all Americans have an equal chance to succeed and none have special privileges. On the other hand, more than two-thirds of us are willing to tell interviewers that we personally belong to a particular class—usually either the middle class or the working class.

However ambiguous our feelings may be, there is no doubt that status or class groupings do exist in American society and behave differently in politics. For example, from the early 1930s through the 1950s the rule was simple: higher-status people voted heavily Republican, and lower-status people, predominantly Democratic. In the 1960s and 1970s, however, the picture has become somewhat more complicated as is shown in Table 3.

The patterns in Table 3 show that all of the status groups have shifted somewhat since the 1950s. Upper-status white Southerners are still Democrats, but less so; upper-status Northern WASPS (white Anglo-Saxon Protestants) are still Republicans, but less so; lower-status Southerners and Northerners are still Democrats, but are more independent; and only blacks, the lowest-status group of all, are even more Democratic than they were in the 1950s.[6]

[6] Cf. Jeane J. Kirkpatrick, "Changing Patterns of Electoral Competition," in Anthony King (ed.), *The New American Political System,* American Enterprise Institute for Public Policy Research, Washington, D.C., 1978, pp. 251–276.

TABLE 3 Partisanship and opinion profiles of social groups in the 1950s and 1970s

| | 1950s | | 1970s | |
Group	Issues	Party	Issues	Party
Middle- and upper-status native white Southerners	Quite a bit to the right	Strongly Democratic	Move further right	Move away from Democratic party, more Independent
Lower-status native white Southerners	Moderately right	Strongly Democratic	Move further right	Move away from Democratic party, more Independent
High-status Northern WASP	Moderately right	Strongly Republican	Move a bit left and splits	Less Republican, more Independent
Middle- and lower-status Northern WASP	Center	Slightly Republican	Move a bit right	More Independent and more Democratic
Blacks	Strongly left	Strongly Democratic	Move even further left	Even more Democratic
Catholics	Moderately left	Strongly Democratic	Move to center	A bit more Independent
Jews	Strongly left	Strongly Democratic	Move further left	A bit more Independent
Border South	Moderately right	Strongly Democratic	Move a bit further right and split a bit	More Independent

Source: Norman H. Nie, Sidney Verba, and John R. Petrocik, *The Changing American Voter*, Harvard University Press, Cambridge, Mass., 1976, Table 14.10, p. 268.

Yet some rich people have always voted Democratic, and a substantial number of poor people have voted Republican. Apparently, then, one's socioeconomic status is not now, and has never been, a certain indicator of one's politics. One major reason for this is the widespread phenomenon of "class misidentification."

First, however, the two related but distinct kinds of status groupings in American society must be recognized. *Socioeconomic status* consists of one's position in a hierarchy of social prestige and privilege determined by such ojective criteria as income and formal education and such more subjective considerations as the prestige of one's job (doctors high, bartenders low) and the "tone" of the neighborhood in which one lives ("posh" suburbs high, the "wrong side of the tracks" low).

Social class, on the other hand, consists of the social status one *thinks* he or she has. This distinction has both psychological and political significance, for it is not at all uncommon for people to "misidentify" their social class. That is, many people think of themselves as occupying a socioeconomic status other than what a sociologist would assign to them on the basis of the usual objective criteria. A typical version of this phenomenon might be a grocery clerk who left school after the fifth grade, makes $9,000 a year, lives in a declining neighborhood near the gas works, and tells an interviewer that he is, of course, a member of the middle class.

This sort of class misidentification results in part from the fact that Americans are not relegated socially to discrete pigeonholes; rather, they are spread along a social continuum, and the differences between one point and the next are blurred at best. Most of us, moreover, belong in the middle ranges of the continuum rather than at its extremes. Also, many of us are "upwardly mobile," and some of us "downwardly mobile." The overall result is that we live in a far less rigid caste structure than that of, say, India or even Great Britain. Most "misidentifiers" are socially crosspressured, in that their occupation gives them one class identification and their social milieu and neighborhood give them another. The more politically involved they are, however, the more they act like members of the class they *think* they belong to rather than like other people sharing their actual socioeconomic level.

The degree of "class conflict" in American politics varies considerably with the times. It is highest during times of depression or widespread fear of depression and lowest during periods of prosperity. It is intensified when the voters see the competing candidates as representatives of different classes (e.g., Dewey and Truman) and softened when the candidates are not thought to be the spokesmen of particular classes (e.g., Eisenhower and Stevenson).[7] But election-in, election-out, class divisions remain one of the most distinct patterns in American politics.

Ethnic groups "Ethnic" identity is a compound of race, religion, national origin, and the recency of the individual's or the individual's family's migration to America. Conflict among ethnic groups is a prominent feature of the politics of many nations (e.g., French versus English in Canada, Flemings versus Walloons in Belgium, Indians versus blacks in East Africa), but in no nation is it so many-sided, persistent, and visible as in the United States. Thus, party leaders strive always for "balanced tickets"; one of the facts of political life, they say, is that if you have a lot of Irish and Jews in your district, you had better have both an O'Connor and a Goldberg or their equivalents among your candidates. Political commentators tell us that both parties follow a pro-Israel foreign policy today because the "Jewish vote" is large and the "Arab vote" negligible. And most observers feel that the "Catholic" and "anti-Catholic" blocs played critical

[7] Cf. *The American Voter,* pp. 346–368.

roles in the 1960 presidential election. In short, it is apparently impossible to discuss our politics without referring to conflict among ethnic groups.[8]

The voting behavior studies confirm the importance of ethnic divisions. They show that the general pattern since the 1930s has been that the high-status WASPs vote predominantly Republican, and the low-status "minority groups," particularly the Catholics, Jews, and blacks and to a lesser degree the Irish, Poles, and Italians, vote mainly Democratic. The figures in Tables 2 and 3 illustrate these tendencies. Unlike other low-status groups, however, some minority groups are more active politically than the WASPs; Catholics and Jews, for example, have fewer nonvoters than Protestants, although blacks have many more nonvoters than whites.

The voting studies have also found that the most solidly Democratic and most active members of minority groups are those who are most conscious of their ethnic identity, most aware of the group's inferior status, and most resentful of discrimination against its members in housing, jobs, access to high public office, and the like. Conversely, the more "assimilated" the members of a minority group feel—and this depends mainly on how they are actually treated—the more likely they are to divide evenly between the two parties. The intensity of "ethnic politics," then, constitutes an index of how well we are currently living up to our professed national belief that "all men are created equal."

PRIMARY-GROUP MEMBERSHIPS

The most direct and most powerful social influences on voting behavior are those exerted by primary groups, especially families and friends. For many people, of course, primary-group influences press in the same direction as do categoric- and secondary-group influences. Within most families, after all, an occupational, ethnic, and social homogeneity exists. But when categoric- and secondary-group influences work in one direction and primary-group influences in another, the latter usually, though not always, win out.

Husbands and wives   Of all social groups, the most homogeneous politically are husband-wife pairs. The studies show that in 90 to 95 percent of all pairs, the two partners have the same preferences, a solidarity unmatched by any other type of group.[9] The movement for independent political action by women in recent years may have lessened this homogeneity, but it is still greater in husband-wife pairs than in other social groups.

Parents and children   The figures in Table 4 show that when parents are united in their party preference, their children are very likely to acquire that preference. When the parents have differing preferences, the child-

---

[8] Mark R. Levy and Michael S. Kramer, *The Ethnic Factor: How America's Minorities Decide Elections*, Simon & Schuster, Inc., New York, 1973.

[9] Cf. Angus Campbell, Gerald Gurin, and Warren E. Miller, *The Voter Decides*, Harper & Row, Publishers, Incorporated, New York, 1954, p. 203; and *The People's Choice*, p. 141.

TABLE 4 The "hereditary vote": percentage of intergenerational resemblance in partisan orientation, politically active and inactive homes, 1958

Party Identification of offspring	One or both parents were politically active			Neither parent was politically active		
	Both parents were Democrats	Both parents were Republicans	Parents had no consistent partisanship	Both parents were Democrats	Both parents were Republicans	Parents had no consistent partisanship
Strong Democrat	50	5	21	40	6	20
Weak Democrat	29	9	26	36	11	15
Independent	12	13	26	19	16	26
Weak Republican	6	34	16	3	42	20
Strong Republican	2	37	10	1	24	12
Apolitical	1	2	1	1	1	7
	100	100	100	100	100	100

Source: Angus Campbell, Philip E. Converse, Warren E. Miller, and Donald E. Stokes, *The American Voter,* John Wiley & Sons, Inc., New York, 1969, Table 7-1, p. 147.

ren are also divided. When the parents are divided in preference *and* politically inactive, the children's preferences are evenly spread across the entire scale. Inactive parents with no consistent partisanship produce the most politically apathetic children.

The tendency to a "hereditary vote," then, is strong. Yet a number of factors can work against it. For instance, persons whose socioeconomic status is substantially higher than their Democratic parents' status are more likely to vote Republican than persons whose socioeconomic status remains the same as that of their Democratic parents. Still, the strength of the "hereditary vote" is shown by the fact that the former are more likely to vote Democratic than other persons in their status group whose parents were both Republicans. The authors of *Voting,* indeed, found that "most" of the deviants in class voting can be explained in terms of the father's traditional vote.[10] About two-thirds of upper-socioeconomic-status Democrats and lower-socioeconomic-status Republicans were voting in line with their fathers.[11]

Peer groups Our peer groups—friends and coworkers—tend to be almost, but not quite, as politically homogeneous as our families. The Berelson research group, for example, asked their respondents to describe the party preferences of their three best friends and of the three coworkers they knew best.[12] Only one in five Republican respondents

[10]Bernard R. Berelson, Paul F. Lazarsfeld, and William N. McPhee, *Voting,* The University of Chicago Press, Chicago, 1954, p. 90.
[11]Bruce A. Campbell, *The American Electorate,* Holt, Rinehart and Winston, New York, 1979, pp. 111–113.
[12]*Voting,* pp. 93–101.

named as many as one Democrat in either group, and only two in five Democrats named as many as one Republican. As would be expected, those who numbered one or more members of the opposition among their associates are more cross-pressured than those who did not. Of those whose friends were all Republicans, 88 percent voted Republican, and 85 percent of those whose friends were all Democrats voted Democratic; but those who had one Democratic and two Republican friends voted only 74 percent Republican, and those who had two Democratic and one Republican friend voted only 52 percent Republican.

In summary, then, our immediate personal environment is largely undisturbed by the sharp political dissension that, according to the newspapers, is continual in the national arena. Our families, our friends, and our coworkers provide most of us with a political atmosphere of mutual agreement and reinforcement. They do not often challenge us to defend our views or plead with us to change them; rather they support us and show us how right we are.

Any one of us, therefore, would find it extremely painful to abandon this warm and secure comfort for the lonely and demanding posture of "standing on principle" at the cost of hurting our parents and angering our friends. Perhaps that is why primary groups shape our voting behavior more powerfully than do any of the other social groups to which we belong.

COMMUNICATIONS PROCESSES

The group influences heretofore discussed are brought to bear on the voter from the external world by a set of processes called "communications." The most significant of these are the following:

Mass communications These include the messages transmitted by such media as newspapers, television, radio, movies, magazines, pamphlets, and even books. All are literally "broadcast"—beamed at large numbers of receivers who are not individually known to the senders. The senders learn the receivers' reactions to the messages only some time after they have been sent, and then only by such incomplete evidence as letters to the editor, audience ratings of television shows, and newspaper and magazine circulation figures.

The American people are avid consumers of mass communications. Some 90 percent of us read some part of a daily newspaper, more than 97 percent of all homes have television sets and in the average home the set is turned on six hours a day, and the average American watches three hours of television each day.[13] How much of this heavy, if not always nourishing, diet is political? A little more than half the pages of daily newspapers are devoted to advertising, and of the remaining "news space" about a quarter is devoted to governmental affairs. Television gives only about 5 percent of its time to news in general, and 1.5 percent to the discussion of public issues. Thus the proportion of directly political content

[13]Statistical Abstract of the United States, 1977, Bureau of the Census, Washington, D.C., 1977, Table 960, p. 583; and Public Opinion, August–September 1979, p. 28.

in mass communications is relatively small, although the absolute amount is as much or more than most of us can digest.

What are the effects of mass communications on voting behavior?[14] For one thing, they provide most of the entries for the voters' cognitive maps, but not much of the affective coloring: About three-quarters of the nation's press consistently favors the Republicans, and yet the Democrats continue to be the majority party. Mass communications do, however, furnish much of the material from which voters build their mental pictures of political reality.

In addition, the people most likely to be swayed by mass communications are, ironically, the people who give them the least attention. A number of studies have shown that people who are the most interested and involved politically pay the most attention to political discussions in the mass media. And, as we have seen, these people are also the most partisan, the most set in their preferences, and therefore the least likely to be "converted" by anything they see on television or read in a newspaper. The people who might be converted, on the other hand, usually switch channels when a political speech or a public affairs program comes on and skip past the political news on the front page to get the sports and comics.

The partisan viewers and readers, moreover, for the most part "tune in" only messages from the side they favor and "tune out" the opposition. Consequently, most political mass communications convey pep talks to the faithful, not arguments to convert the heathen.

This does *not* mean, be it noted, that mass communications are politically without influence and not worth the many millions of dollars parties and pressure groups spend on them. It means only that their main effect is to prevent the faithful from defecting and, most important of all, to get them sufficiently excited that they will get themselves to the polls on Election Day.

This, then, is the general role of mass communication in American politics. The most revolutionary innovations in recent years have been the Kennedy-Nixon television and radio debates in the 1960 presidential campaign and the similar Carter-Ford debates in the 1976 campaign. These occasions were the first in history in which the two major-party presidential candidates engaged in face-to-face discussions on the same platform before a common audience. In 1960 the total audience was estimated at 107 million adults, and in 1976 it was 122 million—over 80 percent of the electorate in both years, and by far the largest audiences ever to hear political discussions of any kind in this country.

In these debates, contrary to the usual pattern noted previously, each candidate's partisans could hardly avoid listening to the other candidate, and direct comparisons between the candidates were possible as never before. A number of studies have concluded that the debates had a con-

[14]The most authoritative surveys of this complex subject include Joseph T. Klapper, *The Effects of Mass Communication,* The Free Press, New York, 1960; Sidney Kraus and Dennis Davis, *The Effects of Mass Communication on Political Behavior,* Pennsylvania State University Press, University Park, Pa., 1978; and Thomas E. Patterson and Robert McClure, *The Unseeing Eye,* G. P. Putnam's Sons, New York, 1976.

siderable impact on the voters. In both years they supplied many voters with most of the information they had on the candidates' personal qualities and stands on the issues. In 1960 they helped Kennedy win his narrow victory over Nixon by depriving Nixon of his initial advantage in being presumed to have greater experience and knowledge than Kennedy. And in 1976 they helped Ford to reduce Carter's large initial lead, although they were not enough to overtake it.[15] The future format and status of presidential campaign debates is in doubt, but the 1960 and 1976 debates clearly provided a dramatic example of the role mass communication can play in voting behavior.

Interpersonal discussion   A number of studies have shown that about three-quarters of all adults occasionally discuss political affairs with their associates. Most interpersonal political discussion consists of comments on events reported in the mass media, and a good deal of it is about politically important *people* rather than public issues. One of the most popular topics, indeed, is the latest newspaper or television charge that this or that public figure has been caught with his hand in the public till.

Very little interpersonal political discussion consists of debate between persons of different preferences. Almost all takes place within well-established primary groups, and these, as we have seen, are for the most part politically homogeneous. Consequently, most political talk consists of the exchange of what might be called "heated agreements" rather than "hot disputes." Political controversy, in short, is much rarer in the living room or over the back fence than it is on the front page.[16]

Yet, when political disagreements do sometimes arise, primary groups usually make conscious efforts to bring the straying sheep back into the fold. Often they succeed. All of us, after all, need the approval and affection of our families and friends. And so, if need be, we will either agree or at least keep quiet about our deviant views.

Opinion leaders and the "two-step flow"[17]   Most students of political communication believe that the mass media's political information and ideas do not reach most persons in a "one-step flow" direct from the media. Rather they are communicated by a "two-step flow": first from the mass media to opinion leaders, and then from the opinion leaders to other persons in their primary groups. The evidence suggests that in most primary groups there are one or two individuals who are especially interested in politics, "consume" an unusually large proportion of the mass media's political content, and initiate most of their particular group's political discussions. Thus opinion followers (which includes most persons)

---

[15]The main discussions of the organization and impact of the 1960 and 1976 debates are Sidney Kraus (ed.), *The Great Debates,* Indiana University Press, Bloomington, Ind., 1962; and Austin Ranney (ed.), *The Past and Future of Presidential Debates,* American Enterprise Institute for Public Policy Research, Washington, D.C., 1979.

[16]*Voting,* pp. 102-109.

[17]The leading discussions are Elihu Katz, "The Two-Step Flow of Communication: An Up-to-Date Report on an Hypothesis," *Public Opinion Quarterly,* vol. 21, pp. 61-78, 1957; and Elihu Katz and Paul F. Lazarsfeld, *Personal Influence,* The Free Press, New York, 1955.

acquire much of their information and many of their ideas from personal discussions with the opinion leaders in their families, work-associate groups, and friendship circles.

Political opinion leaders are generally like the other members of their primary groups, only a bit more so; that is, they are of the same social status, occupation, and ethnic group as their fellows, but they are somewhat better educated. They are also more involved in politics, they pay more attention to the political content of the mass media, and they are better informed.

Rarely do opinion leaders "give the word" with the conscious purpose of shaping their associates' opinions. They are simply interested in politics, and when they get together with their friends and neighbors they just naturally talk politics as others talk football or gardening or movies. Their associates listen because they like and respect the opinion leaders, because they want to *be* liked and respected by them—and because it is very useful to have someone they know and trust explain to them the confusing and rather boring political to-do in the papers. The authors of *Voting* well sum it up as follows:

> The principal agencies [shaping voting behavior] are not Machiavellian manipulators, as is commonly supposed when bloc votes are delivered at the polls, but the ordinary family, friends, co-workers and fellow organization members with whom we are all surrounded. In short, the influences to which voters are most susceptible are opinions of trusted people expressed to one another.[18]

REVIEW QUESTIONS

1 What "reference groups," if any, politically influence you most? Does this also hold true for your family and friends, and are there any differences worth mentioning?

2 To what extent do your own voting preferences and activity resemble those of the majority of your sex, age group, educational group, ethnic group, and social class?

3 Did you watch or hear any of the Carter-Ford debates in 1976? If so, what, if anything, did you learn from them that affected your view of the two candidates? Do you think such debates ought to be made compulsory in every presidential campaign?

4 What role do ethnic groups play in elections in your hometown? In your state?

5 Do you personally know anyone whose political views and voting behavior differ sharply from those of his or her parents? If so, how do you account for the differences?

[18]*Voting,* p. 115. See also ibid., pp. 109–114; and *Personal influence.* For a critical appraisal of the "two-step flow" idea, see Kraus and David, *The Effects of Mass Communication on Political Behavior,* pp. 9–131.

6 How much do you talk politics? With whom? How often do you argue with people who disagree with you?

7 Do you know anyone who fits the general description of "the opinion leader" given in the text? If so, what is the source of this person's own opinions and facts? How much and in what ways does he or she influence the views of other people?

8 The widely read book by Joe McGinnis, *The Selling of the President 1968* (Trident Press, New York, 1969) says in effect that in 1968 Richard Nixon was "packaged" and "sold" to the American people by advertising agencies hired by the Republican party and that is why he won. Do you think this is essentially correct? Why or why not? How powerful a weapon do you think political advertising is generally?

3 POLITICS OF VOTING

Psychologists study voting behavior to learn about human behavior. Sociologists study it to help them understand the influence of social institutions on behavior. Both disciplines view the distributions of the voters' preferences and activity as "dependent variables," that is, as *results* of the forces they are studying. Consequently, both quite properly focus on what *causes* individual and group voting patterns, and electoral patterns are the end products of the processes they are interested in.

Not so political scientists. Although they gratefully accept from psychologists and sociologists information on voters, voting patterns constitute the beginning of their studies. For they see these patterns as one set of factors that mold the governing system and determine the distribution of political power.

PATTERNS OF TURNOUT

Voting "turnout" refers to the proportion of persons of legal voting age who actually vote in a given election. The question of how much nonvoting is unhealthy for a democracy has long concerned political theorists, and the question of which party is the more damaged by the stay-at-homes persistently troubles politicians.

By types of election   The turnout rate in the United States varies considerably according to the type of election. Turnout is almost invariably lower in primary elections than in general elections. One set of evidence for this statement is given in Table 5, which shows that turnout in contested primary elections for governor and United States senator in the period 1962–1976 (line 3 in Table 5) was only about half as large as that in the ensuing general elections. Even where both parties' primaries were contested (line 1 in Table 5) the turnout was only three-fifths as large as that in the general elections.

The same pattern is strikingly evident in presidential primaries and elections. For example, in the ninety-three presidential primaries held from 1948 through 1972 the mean turnout was only 27 percent, compared with a mean turnout of 61 percent in the ensuing presidential elections in the same states—a falloff of 34 percentage points. Only eleven of those primaries had major contests in both parties, and their turnout

TABLE 5 Mean voting turnout in primary and general elections for governor and United States senator, 1962–1976 (percent)

	For governor			*For senator*		
Contests	*Primary elections*	*General elections*	*Difference*	*Primary elections*	*General elections*	*Difference*
Both parties' primaries contested	31.3	51.4 (N = 124)	–22.1	28.6	51.3 (N = 113)	–22.7
Only one party's primary contested	21.7	50.8 (N = 79)	–29.1	17.5	50.5 (N = 106)	–33.0
Lines 1 and 2 combined	27.6	51.4 (N = 203)	–23.8	23.2	50.9 (N = 219)	–27.7
Neither party's primary contested		(N = 20)			(N = 31)	

Source: Primary and general election returns are taken from Richard M. Scammon (ed.), *America Votes*, Elections Research Center and Congressional Quarterly, Inc., Washington, D.C., volumes for 1962, 1964, 1966, 1968, 1970, 1972, 1974, and 1976. Estimates of voting-age populations in each state are taken from *Statistical Abstract of the United States 1977*, Bureau of the Census, Washington, D.C., 1977, Table 818, p. 510.

averaged 39 to 60 percent in the ensuing general elections—a falloff of 30 percentage points.[1]

The 1976 election should have been a bumper year for voting in presidential primaries. Primaries were held in twenty-eight states, the largest number in history up to that time, and there were major contests in both parties in twenty-four of them. But the turnout in the contested primaries was only 29 percent, compared with 53 percent in the general election. Thus the falloff was 24 percentage points, down somewhat from the earlier period but only because of the sharp drop in the general election.[2]

In short, no matter what kind of office we are talking about, primary elections attract many fewer voters than general elections. *Why?* The answer seems to be this: For most Americans, as we have seen, their party

[1] The data for 1948–1968 are taken from Austin Ranney, "Turnout and Representation in Presidential Primary Elections," *American Political Science Review*, vol. 66, Table 1, p. 24, 1972. The data for 1972 are taken from Richard M. Scammon (ed.), *America Votes II*, Elections Research Center and Congressional Quarterly, Inc., Washington, D.C., 1975.
[2] Austin Ranney, *Participation in American Presidential Nominations, 1976*, American Enterprise Institute for Public Policy Research, Washington, D.C., 1977, Table 5, p. 25.

PERCENT OF
AGE-ELIGIBLE VOTERS VOTING

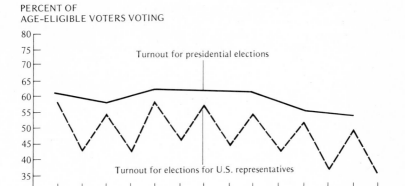

FIGURE 3 Voting turnout for President and United States House of Representatives, 1952-1978. (*Statistical Abstract of the United States 1977*, Bureau of the Census, Washington, D.C., 1977, Table 813, p. 508. Figure for 1978 taken from newspaper reports.)

identifications serve as their principal political cue—their main device for making sense out of the confusing world of politics and deciding who should get their votes. Accordingly, most of them tend to see a general election as a fight between the good guys (the candidates of their party) and the bad guys (the candidates of the other party). And so the choice is clear and unambiguous, and it often seems important to help put the good guys in and/or keep the bad guys out. But in any given primary election, all the candidates belong to the same party; there are no party labels on the ballot distinguishing one from another; and thus there is no clear indication of who are the good guys and who are the bad. Hence the voter's choice is much more ambiguous and much harder to make in a primary than in a general election. As a result, the voters in a party's primary are not any more strongly party-identified than those who skip the primary but rally to the flag in the general election; but they are better educated, more involved in politics, and more knowledgeable about public affairs.[3]

Another marked turnout pattern is the tendency for voting rates to be higher in elections for chief executives than in elections for members of legislative bodies; and turnout in the latter is usually higher in "presidential years" than in "off years," as is shown graphically by Figure 3. This figure shows three striking patterns. First, turnout for President is invariably higher than the turnout for United States representatives. Second, the turnout for representatives is sharply higher in the years in which there is a presidential election than in those in which there are congressional

[3] For analyses of how primary electorates resemble and differ from those in general elections, see Austin Ranney and Leon D. Epstein, "The Two Electorates: Voters and Non-Voters in a Wisconsin Primary," *Journal of Politics,* vol. 28, pp. 598-616, 1966; and Austin Ranney, "The Representativeness of Primary Electorates," *Midwest Journal of Political Science,* vol. 12, pp. 224-238, 1968.

elections only. (This pattern is paralleled in most states by turnouts that are regularly higher in elections for governor than in legislative elections.) And third, turnout in both types of national elections has been declining since 1960, with the sharpest drop coming after the adoption of the eighteen-year-old vote amendment in 1972.

Turnout is almost always higher in national elections than in state and local elections. One sometimes hears it said that state and local governments are "closer" to the people than the national government. Perhaps so, but turnout figures suggest that the people themselves do not see it so. The differentials in turnout according to level of government are greatest in the New England states and smallest in the South, but everywhere the turnout in elections for state or local officers rarely matches or even approaches that in elections for national officers.

By densities of population   In most national and state elections, the metropolitan areas have the largest turnouts, the small towns have the next largest, and the rural areas have by far the lowest. No doubt this is in part a result of the greater practical difficulties in voting resulting from distances and bad weather, but a more powerful factor is the low political involvement of rural people stemming from their isolation from social contacts and political discussion.[4]

By social strata   Certain social strata are correlated with voting turnout: men vote proportionately more than women, older people more than younger people, more educated people more than less educated, people with high socioeconomic status more than people with low status, Catholics and Jews more than Protestants, and whites more than blacks.

By legal handicaps   Undoubtedly some nonvoting results not from apathy but from legal or extralegal handicaps of the sort described in Chapter 1. But how much? In 1976, a total of about 81,551,000 votes was recorded for President. This figure represents 54.4 percent of the estimated adult population of 150,041,000. By no means all of the 68,490,000 adults who did not vote in 1976, however, were people who could easily have voted but did not care to. Scholars have estimated that about 2 percent of the votes cast in presidential elections are regularly invalidated by election officials for improper marking or other reasons; in 1976 this meant a loss of nearly 2 million votes.[5] It is also estimated that about another 9 percent of the voting-age population are effectively prevented from voting by the various impediments put in their way by the states' voting registration laws.[6] In 1976 this meant a loss of another 13,500,000 voters. If these estimates are correct, then perhaps a more meaningful turnout estimate for 1976 would be 65 percent of those for whom it was relatively easy to vote.

[4] Angus Campbell, Philip E. Converse, Warren E. Miller, and Donald E. Stokes, *The American Voter,* John Wiley & Sons, Inc., New York, 1960, pp. 409–416.

[5] *Ibid.,* pp. 94–95.

[6] Steven J. Rosenstone and Raymond E. Wolfinger, "The Effect of Registration Laws on Voter Turnout," *American Political Science Review,* vol. 72, pp. 22–45.

By motivational patterns Even so, nearly 53 million Americans could have voted relatively easily in 1976 but did not. Why not? One recent study of nonvoters shows that they have quite different reasons. The largest number are "positive apathetics"—people who don't bother to vote because their personal lives are going well, they think both candidates are good men, and they are confident that things will continue to go well for them regardless of who is elected; hence, why bother to vote? The next largest number are the "politically impotent"—people who feel that their votes simply do not affect how the government is run; most of them have relatively little education, low incomes, and little knowledge of or interest in politics of any kind. The third group consists of people who would like to vote but are barred by registration difficulties, physical handicaps, or ill health. A fourth group is made up of the "naysayers"—people who deliberately refrain from voting as an act of protest against what they see as the meaninglessness of the choices and the corruption of the whole system. Finally, there are the "cross-pressured"—people who feel some strong pressures to vote Democratic and others to vote Republican, and who resolve the conflict by not voting at all.

Some of the nonvoters, especially the "positive apathetics," do vote sometimes, particularly in presidential elections, often as a favor to a husband, a parent, or a friend. But most of them, for their different reasons, are not likely to vote regularly or in large numbers until and unless they come to feel that voting for a particular party or candidate will help them a lot to get some of the things they want out of life—or to keep some bad things from happening to them.[7]

PATTERNS OF PREFERENCE

Maintaining, deviating, and realigning elections[8] In any election, the individual's voting decision results from his or her consideration of certain short-run situations in relation to his or her long-run predispositions. The latter include such psychological "sets" as the individual's basic cognitive map and party identification and such social influences as sex, ethnic identity, education, socioeconomic status, and the pressures from primary groups. Any change in the content and effects of these long-run forces is likely to be gradual.

The short-run considerations, on the other hand, change much more rapidly, and vary considerably from one election to the next. They include such social and political elements as world or domestic affairs, the candidates, and the concentration of attention on these by the mass communications media. They also include such psychological elements as the voter's perceptions of and feelings about the state of affairs, the issues, and the candidates.

[7] Arthur T. Hadley, The Empty Polling Booth, Prentice-Hall, Inc., Englewood Cliffs, N.J., 1978.
[8] This analysis follows, with some modifications, that in Angus Campbell, Philip E. Converse, Warren E. Miller, and Donald E. Stokes, Elections and the Political Order, John Wiley & Sons, Inc., New York, 1966, chap. 4.

Now if, in a given election, the short-run factors impel the voter toward the same choice as that indicated by his or her long-run predispositions, the voter will almost certainly vote for the candidates of his or her preferred party. But if many of the short-run forces run powerfully counter to the voter's predispositions, he or she is more likely to vote for some or all of the opposition party's candidates.

And so it is with entire electorates, and thus American elections may usefully be classified as one or another of the following three basic types:

A *maintaining election* is one in which the long-standing dominant party wins. The state of affairs, the issues, and the quality of the candidates may help the dominant party, or at worst they are not sufficiently unfavorable to induce enough defections of the faithful to bring defeat. Some recent examples are the congressional elections since 1954 and the presidential elections of 1944, 1964, and 1976.[9]

A *deviating election* is one in which the short-run forces produce enough defections among the adherents of the long-standing dominant party to give victory to the second party. Most of these defectors, however, retain their previous party identifications and may be expected to "return home" when the issues or candidates of the moment have passed. The presidential elections of 1952, 1956, 1968, and 1972 are outstanding recent examples of this type.

A *realigning election* is one in which not only does the second party win but also the basic distribution of party identifications shifts sufficiently to make it the new majority party. Such a shift, of course, takes place over a period of time longer than one election campaign. Yet in each such "realigning era" there is a particular election that marks the turn of the tide. The most recent example is the presidential election of 1932, which marked the accession of the Democratic party to the dominant national position it has held ever since.[10]

Sectionalism: stability and change   As noted in Chapter 1, one of the most prominent patterns in American politics is the continuing loyalty of certain sections of the nation to one party. The "Solid South" from 1880 to 1948 is the best known, but the one-party and modified one-party states described in Chapter 4 are also examples. Their counterparts can be found in some counties in every state, in some cities in every county, and in some precincts in every city. Indeed, our vaunted national "two-party system" results more from a net balance among the two parties' one-party strongholds than from close competition between the parties spread evenly across the nation.

Like the party identifications of individuals, then, the party loyalties of particular sections constitute one of the most stable forces in American politics. Yet as individuals sometimes change their politics, so do sections. Among the more significant political developments of recent years

---

[9]The Center for Political Studies describes the 1960 election as "reinstating," presumably a subtype of "maintaining": cf. Philip E. Converse, Angus Campbell, Warren E. Miller, and Donald E. Stokes, "Stability and Change in 1960: A Reinstating Election," *American Political Science Review,* vol. 55, pp. 269–280, 1961.

[10]Cf. V. O. Key, Jr., "A Theory of Critical Elections," *Journal of Politics,* vol. 17, pp. 3–18, 1955.

have been the increased successes of the second parties in a number of previously one-party areas. Both parties have benefited nationally. The rise of the Democrats in Maine, Oregon, and the High Plains states have been matched by the rise of the Republicans in Arizona, Florida, Texas, and even in Alabama and Mississippi.

Some commentators have suggested that massive switches in the party identifications of the natives produce these section shifts, but this seems highly unlikely. Although some people are indeed changing their party identification, these changes are taking place in both partisan directions, and neither party is showing a national "net profit" of any great significance. Moreover, truly massive switches of party identification occur only in times of great crisis, such as the 1929 Depression.[11] The occurrence most like such a crisis during the recent period of sectional shifts is the bitter controversy in the South over racial desegregation; and although this may account in part for the rise of Republican strength there, it does not explain shifts in other sections.

A better explanation is probably the great intersectional migration that has taken place in the United States since World War II; for whenever large numbers of people migrate from A to B they not only alter the composition of B's population but A's as well. The Center for Political Studies has found that 40 percent of all Americans have moved from one region to another. The greatest migration, of course, has been to the Far West. The statistic that 48 percent of the West's present population grew up in some other region is dramatized by California's rise from being the fifth-most-populous state in 1940 to the most populous in the 1980s.

The Center for Political Studies found that the Northern migrants to the West are predominantly Republican and that the Southern migrants are mainly Democratic. As the former outnumber the latter by two to one, the net effect is to make this formerly heavily Democratic region more evenly divided between the two parties. It may well account for the great recent upsurge of Republican strength led by Senator Barry Goldwater in traditional Democratic Arizona.

Other noteworthy recent population trends are the continuing migration of Southern blacks to the North and of a smaller number of Northern whites to the South. Both movements are probably a major factor in the growth of Republican strength in Florida and Texas.[12]

Country, small town, big city, and suburb   Another long-standing prominent pattern in American politics is the differential voting behavior of Northern areas with different densities of population. Since the late 1920s, generally speaking, the big cities have been heavily Democratic and the small towns heavily Republican, and the rural areas have been Democratic when farm prices are low and Republican when they are high. Thus, elections in each of a number of large Northern states have traditionally been contests between the Democratic metropolitan area and the Republican areas in the rest of the state, e.g., New York City ver-

---

[11] Cf. Bernard R. Berelson, Paul F. Lazarsfeld, and William N. McPhee, *Voting,* The University of Chicago Press, Chicago, 1954, pp. 132–142; and *The American Voter,* pp. 149–167.

[12] Cf. *The American Voter,* pp. 444–453.

sus "upstate" in New York, and Cook County versus "downstate" in Illinois.

Since World War II, the suburbs have become a significant new political factor. Higher incomes have resulted in movement from big cities to suburbs, in which populations have mushroomed while the core populations of the cities in many cases have actually declined. The suburbs supported Eisenhower by large-enough margins in 1952 and 1956 to swing into the Republican column such traditionally Democratic metropolitan areas as New York, Chicago, and Boston. Some commentators declared that the "ex-urbanites" had evidently shed their previous Democratic loyalties and acquired their new neighbors' Republicanism as befitting their newly won respectability. This, it was said, was happening to so many people that it might well make the GOP the nation's majority party again.

Several political scientists have tried to test the truth of this proposition. Their task is greatly complicated by the fact that suburbs are far from all being alike; they differ widely in socioeconomic character and voting tendencies. In the Chicago metropolitan area, to take one well-known example, the population of Cicero is largely working class, while the populations of Wilmette and Glencoe are almost entirely upper-middle class; yet all three are technically suburbs of Chicago. The suburbs of most other big cities are similarly variegated.

In an influential study of metropolitan-area voting behavior, the Center for Political Studies in the 1950s identified three main classes of people now living in metropolitan areas: the "ex-urbanites," who have moved from more urban areas to less urban; the "new urbanites," who have moved from less urban areas to more urban; and the "still-urbanites," who have remained in the same urban areas in which they were reared or have moved from one urban area to another. The ex-urbanites, the Center found, are indeed heavily Republican. They are *not*, however, former Democrats who switched after moving to the suburbs; rather, they were Republicans when they lived in the cities and have remained so after moving to the suburbs. The new urbanites are also heavily Republican, although their general socioeconomic status is much lower than that of the ex-urbanites. The still-urbanites, however, are even more heavily Democratic than the other groups are Republican, and they continue to be the core of the Democratic party's strength outside the South.[13]

The nation's twenty largest cities contribute about 16 percent of the votes cast in presidential elections, and their suburbs add about 26 percent, fully a quarter of the national vote. Most of the central cities, as we have seen, usually vote heavily Democratic, but the suburbs tend to switch their votes back and forth between the two major parties from one election to the next in substantially larger proportions than do residents of the central cities, small towns, or rural areas. No party, therefore, can ever afford to count the suburban vote as "in the bag," and the suburbs will continue to be as critical electoral battlegrounds in the 1980s as they were in the 1960s and 1970s.

[13] *Ibid.*, pp. 453–472.

National loyalties in state and local elections One school of political scientists and civic reformers has long argued that state and local politics should be entirely divorced from national politics. After all, they say, there is no Democratic way to pave a street, nor is there any Republican way to organize a school curriculum; and so the party labels and loyalties of national politics should be kept out of state and local affairs. To that end they have urged, with some success, the adoption of such devices as the nonpartisan election of state legislators (as in Nebraska) and elections for governors and other state officials in nonpresidential-election years (as in thirty-seven of the fifty states).

In the 1950s and earlier it seemed that their objective was far from being reached. V. O. Key, Jr., found that in the thirties and forties, when state elections coincided with national, the party that carried a state for President usually, though not always, carried its ticket for state offices as well. Even the states that elected their officials in nonpresidential years had only slightly more autonomy from national trends.[14] For better or worse, it seemed that most people apparently thought of themselves as members of the *national* parties and infrequently set aside those loyalties in elections for state and local offices. Consequently, many state and local elections were reflections of national trends more than responses to special local circumstances. But there are reasons to believe that the situation has changed considerably since Key made his analysis.

Ticket splitting American voters have the world's richest opportunities for "ticket splitting," that is, voting for candidates of both parties in a single election. Federalism gives them two sets of governments to elect officials for, and separation of powers gives them several officials to choose for each set. Consequently, ticket splitting has long been a familiar phenomenon in American politics.

The 1972 elections featured the greatest ticket splitting in American history. Republican incumbent Richard Nixon won the presidency by the third largest landslide in this century, with 60.7 percent of the popular vote and victories in forty-nine of the fifty states. But his personal success helped his party very little in other races. For example, nineteen states also held gubernatorial elections in 1972; Nixon carried all nineteen with an average majority of 62.3 percent, and one might have expected many Republican candidates for governor to ride in on his coattails. But those candidates averaged only 45.9 percent of the vote, and only seven of the nineteen won. Moreover, before the election the Democrats controlled both houses of twenty-four state legislatures; after the election they controlled twenty-six. Much the same happened in congressional elections: the Democrats won 51.7 percent of all votes for United States representatives, dropped only fifteen seats in the House, added two seats in the Senate, and thus maintained the substantial majorities in both houses they have held since the mid-1950s.

[14] V. O. Key, Jr., *American State Politics: An Introduction,* Alfred A. Knopf, Inc., New York, 1956, chap. 2.

Clearly, then, many Americans in 1972 voted for Nixon (or against McGovern) for the Presidency but voted for Democrats for congressional and state offices. Some striking examples: McGovern lost Vermont with 37 percent of the vote, but Democratic Governor Thomas Salmon won with 55 percent; McGovern lost Kansas with 29 percent, but Democratic Governor Robert Docking won with 62 percent; and in the greatest spread of all, McGovern lost Utah with 26 percent while Democratic Governor Calvin Rampton won with 70 percent! And so whatever else may have happened in 1972, state elections were clearly quite independent of the presidential election.

Much the same was true in 1976, although the disparities were not so huge. For example, Jimmy Carter lost Montana with 45 percent of the vote, but Democratic Governor Thomas Judge won reelection with 62 percent; Carter lost North Dakota with 46 percent, but Democratic Governor Arthur Link was reelected with 52 percent. It also worked the other way: Carter carried Delaware with 52 percent, but Democratic Governor Sherman Tribbitt was defeated for reelection, winning only 42 percent.

Such ticket splitting has increased steadily in this century. In the election of 1900 only about 5 percent of the voters voted for candidates of different parties. The figure rose to 35 percent in 1960, 57 percent in 1964, 66 percent in 1968, 67 percent in 1972,[15] and in 1976 the figure stayed about the same. We do not know what has caused this increase in ticket splitting. It may be the people's growing disillusionment with the parties, or it may be the result of civics-textbook teaching that one should vote for individual candidates and not straight party slates, or it may be something else. But we do know that it has become a major factor in American politics and is likely to remain so.

Who are the ticket splitters? The Center for Political Studies found them to be of two main types: the highly involved but cross-pressured voters, who resolve their internal conflicts by dividing their ballots; and the indifferent voters, who cross over for this or that candidate as a favor to a friend or because the candidate is from the neighborhood.[16] The straight-ticket voters are of comparable types: the highly involved, highly partisan voters with no cross-pressures (mainly big-city Democrats and suburban Republicans); and the indifferent voters who vote the straight tickets of their traditional parties because it is too much trouble to do otherwise.

THE AMERICAN VOTER AND THE
AMERICAN WAY OF GOVERNMENT

What impact does this kind of voting behavior have on the American way of government? Do American voters act as the citizens of a democracy should?

[15] Norman H. Nie, Sidney Verba, and John R. Petrocik, *The Changing American Voter,* Harvard University Press, Cambridge, Mass., 1976, Fig. 4.3, p. 53.
[16] Angus Campbell and Warren E. Miller, "The Motivational Basis of Straight and Split Ticket Voting," *American Political Science Review,* vol. 51, pp. 293–312, 1957. See also Walter De Vries and V. Lance Tarrance, *The Ticket Splitter: A New Force in American Politics,* William B. Eerdmans Publishing Co., Grand Rapids, Mich., 1972.

The voters' impact   The voting patterns described constitute one of the major forces (along with such other influences as the Constitution, the political parties, and the pressure groups) that characterize and sustain our political system. They help to produce and maintain its heterogeneity, its complexity, its low ideological content, its high consensus, and above all its "pluralistic" way of making decisions by negotiation and bargaining among many different social groups.

The voters' general impact is more clearly seen when we consider the following:[17]

1 The two-party system   The durable attachment of American voters to the Democratic or Republican party has been the main preservative of our national two-party system. More than any other factor, it explains the historic inability of third parties to acquire enough popular support to create a multiple-party system. The strong and persistent loyalties of particular sections to particular parties, moreover, have kept the nation from becoming a one-party system: they guarantee that each party will have strongholds from which it cannot be dislodged no matter how great a national sweep the other party may make. Accordingly, if the steady weakening of party identification that began in the mid-1960s continues into the 1980s and beyond, it is bound to have a substantial impact upon the stability, even upon the meaning, of the traditional two-party system.

2 Ambiguous "mandates"   The two main spectator sports in American politics are preelection guessing about who will win and postelection speculation about what the results "mean." If the former is difficult, the latter is impossible; for there is no way of telling from *who* wins an election *what* that indicates about the policies the voters now wish the government to follow. This is in part a consequence of the ambiguity and inconsistency of the parties' platforms and the candidates' speeches. It is also a consequence of the low degree of knowledge about and interest in specific policy issues underlying most votes. The only "mandate" an election can give is a mandate for the winners to exercise the powers of their office as best they can until the next election. Yet a *series* of elections can reveal the electorate's predominant feelings about the broad goals the government should pursue and the general direction it should take. Few would doubt, for example, that the presidential elections since 1932, taken together, indicate that a majority of the American electorate wants the national government to take active responsibility for maintaining prosperity and to play an active role in world affairs. But no one can say with any confidence that the election of Jimmy Carter in 1976 was a popular mandate either for or against, say, federal support of schoolteachers' salaries or amnesty for Vietnam war draft-dodgers. The only certainty was that a plurality of the American voters wanted the powers of the Presidency to be exercised by Jimmy Carter rather than by Gerald Ford.

3 Low-pressure politics   In some nations politics is literally a matter of life and death, for it decides who will eat and who will not, and even who

---

[17] Cf. Talcott Parsons, " 'Voting' and the Equilibrium of the American Political System," in Eugene Burdick and Arthur J. Brodbeck (eds.), *American Voting Behavior,* The Free Press New York, 1959, chap. 4.

will get shot and who will do the shooting. In such nations there is no need to tell the people that politics is important and that good citizens should be interested in it; they know it only too well. In the United States, however, most voters are only sporadically interested in politics. They regard voting in an election not as an opportunity to smash or be smashed by the enemy, but rather like going to church on Christmas and Easter: a time to reaffirm loyalty to the faith of one's forebears. Few Americans feel their personal life will be substantially altered by the outcome of an election, and indeed society does seem to carry on afterward much as it did before. Thus high voting turnout is not, by itself, necessarily a sign of a healthy democracy, nor is low voting turnout a sign of a sick democracy: after all, Italy regularly turns out over 90 percent of its voters in national elections, while Switzerland rarely achieves even a 50 percent turnout; yet few would say that democracy is healthy in Italy and sick in Switzerland.

4 Political change All this is *not* to say, however, that American elections do not matter. They do—not because they are ever the sole or even the main causes of significant social change, but because they can make it possible for other causes to operate with maximum impact. Just in recent years, for instance, the Johnson landslide in 1964 produced a Congress which made it possible for Johnson to complete the New Deal's agenda of social legislation. And the 1974 Democratic sweep of Congress made it possible for the forces which had been pressing for internal congressional reform to win after thirty years of losing. Certainly the people who lead our businesses, our unions, our schools, our consumer- and environmental-protection groups, and the like, are not bored by or apathetic about electoral politics. They have no doubt that the nation's elections profoundly affect the values they cherish. And they are right.

The democratic citizen and the American voter The typical American voter falls short of the model citizen of a democracy described by democratic political theorists such as John Locke, Jean Jacques Rousseau, and Thomas Jefferson.

The ideal democratic citizen, for one thing, is highly concerned with public affairs and places high priority on doing his civic duties. The average American voter is only somewhat and sometimes interested in public affairs; the extent of his or her political activity is casting an occasional vote; and often well over half of American adults do not even make that minimal contribution.

For another thing, ideal democratic citizens make rational decisions on the basis of facts. They keep themselves well informed about the principal public issues facing the community, carefully weigh the pros and cons of each of the proposals advanced, and rationally choose that which is best for the community. The typical American voter has only a modest amount of information about public affairs in general and even less about specific policy proposals; his or her conceptual apparatus is simple and crude; and his or her decisions are for the most part merely reaffirmations of traditional loyalties to family, social groups, and political parties as filtered through the views of particular opinion leaders.

For a third thing, ideal democratic citizens test ideologies and policy proposals in "the free market of ideas"; they engage in debate and discussion with citizens of contrary views, and out of this process ultimately emerges a general consensus supporting the ideas which have best passed the tests of the marketplace. The average American voter rarely engages in debate or discussion with people who hold contrary views; he or she talks politics, if at all, with family, friends, and coworkers; and most of the talk consists of the exchange of agreements rather than discussion in the idealized sense.

Finally, the democratic citizen has an unselfish moral code, which he or she applies to public affairs as well as private. The typical American voter acts either from frank self-interest or from loyalty to other people.

The foregoing contrasts between the ideal and the actual are undeniably depressing. What, then, should we conclude? That the ideal of participatory democracy is just as shining and splendid as ever, but that *homo Americanus* is just not up to it? That the ideal is splendid and could be realized if our institutions were made more hospitable to democratic participation?[18] Or that the ideal is too far out of touch with the realities of modern densely populated societies, and that "democracy" in our time must mean government run by small groups of leaders periodically held responsible by the voters in popular elections?[19]

In the present writers' opinion, there is another, better way to view these difficult questions. Remember that the classical democratic theorists constructed their picture of the ideal citizen without reference to the problems of governing an industrially complex and ethnically polyglot nation of more than 200 million people. Accordingly, they concentrated on problems of *articulation,* i.e., how to isolate and clarify ideological differences among the citizens and then count heads to see which ideologies or policies are supported by popular majorities and therefore must be translated into governmental action.

We in the 1980s have one great advantage over the giants of the past. We can reflect on the nearly two centuries of efforts by people in many societies to establish democratic governments. And we have learned that problems of *consensus* are at least as urgent and difficult as problems of articulation. We know that the clarification of differences and measurement of their strength is only half the battle; for if the losers will not peacefully accept the electoral decision, or if the winners persecute the losers for their wrong-headedness, then democracy cannot survive.[20]

In American society the task of maintaining consensus is herculean. No society is occupationally, ethnically, or ideologically more heterogeneous than we. Such political conflicts as the current struggles over racial

---

[18]Leading expositions of the view that participatory democracy is still the desirable and possible goal and that our institutions must be changed to make it possible include Peter Bachrach, *The Theory of Democratic Elitism: A Critique,* Little, Brown and Company, Boston, 1967; and Jack L. Walker, "A Critique of the Elitist Theory of Democracy," *American Political Science Review,* vol. 55, pp. 285–295, 1966.

[19]Leading exponents of the choice-of-elites school include Robert A. Dahl, *A Preface to Democratic Theory,* The University of Chicago Press, Chicago, 1956; and Joseph Schumpeter, *Capitalism, Socialism, and Democracy,* 3d ed., Harper Torchbooks, New York, 1950.

[20]For a fuller exposition of this point of view, see Austin Ranney and Willmoore Kencall, *Democracy and the American Party System,* Harcourt, Brace & World, Inc., New York, 1956, chaps. 2, 3.

desegregation and busing of schoolchildren match any in the world for bitterness and "civil war potential." Consequently, the American political system's achievement of dealing with such issues for more than a century without civil war or violent revolution is surely a great triumph as humanity's civic triumphs are measured.

The pluralism, moderation, and compromise that have made this triumph possible are sustained by many institutions. Our systems of federalism and separation of powers fragment authority so that no single interest can capture the whole power of government and wreak vengeance on the opposition. If Watergate proved anything, it proved this. Our political parties nominate candidates, write platforms, and conduct campaigns in such a manner that we are never faced with clear and inescapable choices between total electoral victory for one side or the other on issues like racial desegregation—electoral victories of the kind that in other nations are usually followed by violent revolutions launched by the losers.

Here too, American voters make a great contribution. Their continuing loyalty to the two major parties gives the system the stability it must have to work out its slow and moderate pluralistic solutions to the problems before us. Yet this stability never becomes ossification. Anyone who believes otherwise should compare the United States of the 1920s with that of the 1980s.

By the same token, the voters' low-pressure concern with politics insures that election losers are not impelled to start revolutions against the winners and that winners are not driven to start shooting the losers. Rather, the atmosphere of limited ambiguity it creates about the meaning of elections permits public officials and interest-group leaders to conduct the between-elections negotiation, bargaining, and compromise that are the very essence of American pluralism.

It comes down to this: typical American voters do *not* contribute a sour note to an otherwise harmonious governing system. They are entirely in tune with the Constitution, the political parties, and all the other institutions that make our way of government what it is.

That way unquestionably bears only a family resemblance to the designs and dreams of the great classical democratic theorists. Yet *it works*. And, incurable pragmatists that we are, we are not likely to want or make any changes in it—including reforming our voting behavior—until we think it has stopped working.

Despite the political turmoil precipitated by Watergate and the war in Vietnam, that time has not yet come.

REVIEW QUESTIONS

1 How unhealthy for American democracy is the persistent low turnout in so many of our elections? What, if anything, do you feel should be done about it?

2 Would you say that the 1980 presidential election was a "maintaining," "deviating," or "realigning" election? Why?

3 What are the one-party Republican areas in your state? What makes them so? What are the one-party Democratic areas? Why are they as they are?

4 Make out the best case you can both for and against the proposition, "In a democracy no good citizen will ever vote for a candidate for public office solely because of that person's party label." Which case seems to you the more convincing? Why?

5 After having studied how and why the American people *do* vote, what, if any, changes would you recommend for our laws controlling the legal qualifications for voting? Why?

6 In view of most Americans' failure to participate in government as much as the classical theory of democracy requires, do you feel that the theory is still correct and the people should be encouraged to live up to it? Or do you feel that the theory should be changed to fit modern conditions? Why?

7 In what respects do you expect American voting behavior in the 1980s to resemble and differ from that in the 1970s?

4 PARTY POLITICS

So far we have examined the voting behavior of the political person. We have considered the importance of how that individual perceives, then constructs, puts together, and carries out ideas. Although the average American voter falls short of the idealized democratic citizen and has a rather low-pressure concern for politics, all is not lost. Many citizens find politics exciting and become active participants in the political process. Other citizens "let George do it," only to find that they don't like what George did! Thus they become active to protect their own interest. Other people are motivated to take an interest in government because it has become the instrument for realizing *individual* and *group values* from space research to social security, from building highways to fluoridating water. Whether one believes in the welfare state or not, politics is inevitable.

The great decisions made by government are not made in a vacuum but are the result of *influence*. A mayor who persuades voters to approve a bond issue and a President who persuades Congress to pass a foreign aid measure are exercising influence. A labor leader who induces a mayor to take action and a farm leader who sells a program to the Secretary of Agriculture are exercising influence. Outdoor advertisers who keep billboard regulation off the statute books are using influence. In the United States very few if any of the major public policy decisions are made centrally by a person or group without consultation of interested parties. Rather, policies are evolved as the byproduct of influences by competitive forces. The remainder of this volume is focused on groups and their relationships to public decision making.

THE MAKING OF PUBLIC POLICY

Determiners of policy   The shaping of public policy in the United States is an infinitely complex matter; programs are formulated and promulgated in more ways than are those in parliamentary systems or monolithic dictatorships. There is a similar fragmentation or dispersion of decision making at the state and local levels. Figure 4 notes the constitutional and private agencies through which programs are developed and that groups are intermediate steps to governmental decisions. The figure is over-

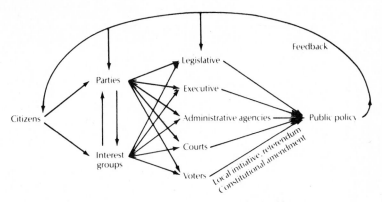

FIGURE 4 Actors and instruments of public decision making.

simplified, for no diagram can show the interrelations and interactions among the legislative, the executive, and the judicial establishments, or the nuances and interplay between voters and interest groups, and between parties and pressure groups. In the states, constitutional amendments proposed by the legislature must be ratified by the voters, and many significant changes come about through this process. The perceptions and values of the decision-makers themselves grow out of their own socialization and vitally affect their votes and decisions.

Most citizens are generally aware of the legislative and executive establishments as determiners of policy. They can point to a law passed by Congress or an action of the President, but they are less cognizant of the important policy decisions of the independent regulatory agencies and diverse state boards. These agencies lay down rules of deep significance in the areas of communication, conservation, transportation, and trade practices. The historic decisions on segregation of the races in the public schools and on "one man, one vote" legislative apportionment have made the present generation aware of the courts' far-reaching decisions. The regulatory agencies and the judiciary are unavoidably involved with politics and many of the great political issues of the times.

Increasing use is being made of lawmaking by the people. In about half of the states voters may bypass the legislature and initiate statutes and/or constitutional amendments. Many states also permit legislatures to refer statutes to the voters or allow voters themselves to request a referendum. In 1978 there were over 350 statewide ballot propositions and hundreds more at the local level. Thirteen states had tax or spending limitations on their ballots, largely as a result of the widely publicized Proposition 13 in California, which drastically reduced property taxes. Ballot measures constitute some of the most exciting political battles in the nation.[1] At times more people vote on them than for some political offices.

[1] For an analysis of the uses and undesirable aspects of initiatives and referendums, see David Butler and Austin Ranney (eds.), *Referendums: A Comparative Study of Practice and Theory,* American Enterprise Institute for Public Policy Research, Washington, D.C., 1978, chap. 2.

Implications of decentralization No one institution formulates public policy; it is derived from fragmented sources. Lack of central direction and decision may mean drift and inaction in some fields. One then looks elsewhere in the government for policy leadership and action. For the person interested in the adoption of a program, the system contains inherent advantages and disadvantages. As there are multiple points of access to constitutional authority—legislative, executive, judicial—defeat in one branch is not necessarily decisive, for the battle may be won in another. Before 1960, black groups won few battles in Congress but were highly successful in the judiciary. Proponents of state ownership of tidelands oil first lost in the courts and through an executive veto, but later won in Congress and obtained a presidential approval. Under a wide but permissive law, a group may find an administrator who will give it at least something. Conversely, citizens have many channels through which to oppose programs. A bicameral legislature affords a chance to kill a measure in the second house. It may be defeated by a veto or a court ruling; or a law may be modified by "flexible" or "sympathetic" enforcement.

The possibility of influencing policy is great, and much money and effort are spent in so doing—the private citizens have an open invitation to negotiate with their government and to participate in pressure-group and party activities. In the American model, citizens have manifold opportunities for playing politics. Their approach need not be exclusively through a political party, pressure group, or citizens' association, though each will give them some influence in and contact with the personnel of government. Neither the parties nor the interest groups have a monopoly on access to government. As they perform different functions, many citizens find it rewarding to be active in both.

For those in public authority, the system requires them to make concessions in order to get action (or inaction). Policy is generally a compromise and a result of the struggle of special interests. There is perhaps some tendency to strengthen the executive because of the need for some centralized responsibility and authority, but executives make few decisions without consultation and concessions.

Decentralization of policy determination makes it difficult for parties to be strongly centralized, either in organization or program. The political parties must make concessions if they are to be victorious at the polls. Similarly, pressure groups find that they too must give in order to get and that no one group gets all its own way all the time.

Forces for integration Perhaps this brief picture looks like multiformity unbounded! But this is not the case—far from it. The institutions provided for in the Constitution have, in rather unique ways, assisted in integrating aspects of political life and helped to build consensus. The extraconstitutional institutions—pressure groups and political parties—are likewise forces for integration and assist in the development of consensus within the context of a pluralist society.

In this and the following chapter we shall look at political parties and electoral politics. The concluding chapter will examine interest-group politics.

WHAT AND WHERE IS A POLITICAL PARTY?

Two centuries ago, the English statesman Edmund Burke spoke approvingly of a political party as "a body of men united for promoting . . . the national interest upon some particular principle on which they all agreed." He felt that parties promoted the public good or the public interest. Several of his contemporaries, including George Washington, were unenthusiastic about political parties. They saw them as infecting the legislature and interfering with efforts to find the public interest. Some regarded parties as necessary evils but admitted that in a free society parties could not be kept from forming.

Socialists have been divided in their attitudes. The totalitarian socialists regard the party as the vanguard of the proletariat. Joseph Stalin said that "class must rule through its head, i.e., the party; it can rule in no other way." Only one party is allowed, and the masses are excluded from membership in it. In contrast, democratic socialists consider competitive parties as a way to bring about socialism and change. The life of the state, they assert, is built upon competitive parties. Parties are brokers of ideas and arrange the issues upon which the people vote.

As they have developed, American major parties have not been operated around the Burkean ideal of unity of principle. Rather, the purpose of parties is to propose candidates for public office and to try to elect them. As such they are pragmatic rather than ideological in outlook and operation. Both encompass a broad spectrum of beliefs and try to build winning coalitions by appealing to the political center. In operation as confederations of individuals and interest groups to gain control of government, the Democrats and Republicans perform various functions and services—with varying degrees of success. They recruit political leaders, provide information, aggregate demands, and attempt to politicize the public. In performance of these duties the party workers conduct research, write platforms, compile voter profiles, answer inquiries, and so on. Many of these service jobs are not exciting but are important to a party's success.

One has problems in finding *the party* in the United States because it has several egos. One may find a committee listing in the phone book. This segment represents the thousands of party officeholders and activists. A second section of the party consists of its officeholders in the executive and legislative branches of the government. This group is often referred to as the "government" party. Third, there are the electorate parties, which are composed of the party's voting adherents and supporters—sometimes denoted as the "party in the country" or the "voters'" party. Tension between the organizational activists and the government parties is rather common, especially in conflict over certain public policies. This tripartite character is a basic concept for understanding the party system in the United States.

THE NATIONAL PARTY SYSTEM

Factors in development George Washington desired a partyless government or a government above parties. No provision was made in the

Constitution for parties, and, except for corrupt-practices laws, the Congress has done little to regulate them. At the state level, however, pressure for mass control has resulted in a considerable volume of legislation-regulating nominating procedures, the selection of party committees, and election practices.

A history of party organization and doctrines cannot be undertaken in this volume,[2] but a few of the great landmarks of party development can be pointed out. Two-party contests for the Presidency did not begin with regularity until 1832, but there was a basis for party struggle from the early days of the Republic, and Federalist candidates vied against Jeffersonian Republicans for the Presidency from 1796 to 1816. The Jeffersonians dreamed of an agrarian society, had faith in the masses, and emphasized states' rights, decentralization, and that the government which governs the least is best. The Federalists saw the industrial society as greatly important and favored using the powers of the central government to promote it. Hamilton favored the dominance of the rich and wellborn. Jefferson's vision of an agrarian America passed from the scene, but his majoritarian ideas won out as politicians embraced them and called upon the government to assist the masses. The early period in the history of the United States saw the Federalists experiencing what so often happens to the opposition party, the taking over of many of their programs by the majority party. Jeffersonians "federalized" a number of programs and did so with a "democratic image." Many Federalists soon found themselves able in good conscience to vote for Republicans.

The period from Jackson to Lincoln was of singular significance to party development. Equalitarian ideas spread, and suffrage radically broadened. Longer ballots and frequent rotation in office made more public jobs available, and politics became the business of a much larger number of citizens. Mass geographical election-district organization was created to reach the increasing number of voters. State and local committees were followed, beginning in 1848, with national committees. National and state conventions replaced caucuses as instruments of nomination. State legislative appointment of presidential electors gave way to selection by popular vote.

The Democratic-Whig era (1828–1860) was significant not only for the development of party organizations to mobilize the party voters in ballyhoo campaigns, but also for the struggle over presidential and legislative power. Both parties reversed their historic positions. The Democrats supported a strong President as the spokesman for popular majorities; and the Whigs, unlike their Federalist ancestors, opposed a strong executive and put their faith in a strong legislature that could be relied upon to curb government activity. With some exceptions, the Democrats have continued to be the party of strong Presidents and the advocate of strong government to curb private power and advance the interests of the less privileged.

A number of changes were necessitated in party practices as a result

[2] For a general history, see W. E. Binkley, *American Political Parties: Their Natural History*, 4th ed., Alfred A. Knopf, Inc., New York, 1963. See also Everett C. Ladd, Jr., *American Political Parties: Social Change and Social Response*, W. W. Norton & Company, New York, 1970.

of the Progressive Movement from 1900 to 1920. Corrupt-practices legislation appeared, and most state and local nominations were moved from conventions to direct primaries. A number of states also required that delegates to national conventions be selected in the primaries. Suffrage was further democratized by the direct election of United States senators and the extension of voting to women (1920). The growth of the merit system deprived party organizations of a number of public jobs.

Another reform surge in the 1960s and 1970s had further impacts on the party system. The poll tax and lengthy residence requirements for voting were abolished. A massive attack was made on registration restrictions which had kept many blacks and some other minorities from voting. This resulted in a spectacular increase in black voters and in the number of black elected officials, especially in the South. The voting age was lowered to eighteen. The Democratic party adopted new rules for its national convention delegates in 1972, greatly increasing the number of delegate seats for the young, minorities, and women. There was a corresponding reduction in the number of public officeholders and old-time political professionals among delegates at the convention. Both parties also made efforts to bring new types of activists into the precinct- and district-level organizations. Other major changes brought about public financing of presidential elections and limitations in the amount of contributions given to an individual candidate for Congress within a single year. Public-disclosure laws also required more information on campaign donations and the personal wealth of public officeholders.

Other aspects   The perspective of history suggests that the major parties have been associated with the concepts of "geographical" and "ideological" parties. At times, each party has been buttressed by a strong sectional base that rested, to a considerable extent, on ideology. Yet no party can hope to win the Presidency if it is exclusively a sectional or ideological party. A party must constantly balance and shift the combination of elements that take cognizance both of geography and of doctrine; increased technology, mobility, and industrialization tend to modify sectionalism, and they have assisted in promoting a nationalization of politics.

Since the beginning of the United States, the major parties have been diversified and heterogeneous in composition. Federalists appealed for and received votes not only from aristocrats and capitalists but also from New York blacks and New England fishermen. The Whig party was a motley combination of "nationalists," states' righters, and Federalists. It is remarkable that negativism, protest, and hope for patronage bound the Whig party together for twenty years and made it capable of winning two elections with popular generals as candidates. To succeed, a party must draw support from all large elements of society. The Federalists' failure to win support from the inland agrarian voters led to the downfall of the party. If a party that is broadly composed can avoid enervating factionalism and keep a fair degree of cohesion among its membership, it will likely remain the victor over the party less well constituted.

History also tells us that those parties that have remained in power adapted themselves to changing times and have been highly pragmatic. Inflexibility in the face of change runs the risk of losing a following to the opposition. Successful strategy also dictates that new majorities, upon assuming control, retain those parts of a predecessor regime that are popular. It is rare, therefore, that turnover of the party in power brings radical change in program save when there is war or emergency, as in 1860 and 1932.

Dynamic leadership by the President is essential if the party in office is to have a coherent program and rally its followers. Jefferson, Jackson, Lincoln, Wilson, and the two Roosevelts illustrate successful presidential party leadership. All except Wilson were able to weld together agglomerations which survived their own terms of office.

Although a two-party system has prevailed since 1832, one party has tended to dominate over long periods. There has almost never been an alternation of power every four years. The Jacksonian Democrats were the majority party for twenty-eight years before 1860. Cleveland and Wilson provided short breaks in a long period of Republican hegemony, and Wilson won largely because of a Republican schism in 1912.

Voter preferences over the years have undergone much change. Roosevelt's New Deal moved voters away from a long-time Republican dominance. Labor, big-city ethnics, low-income workers, the unemployed, and many farmers moved into the Democratic coalition. Business and professional groups, the better-educated and higher-income, and rural America outside the South tended to remain Republican. These coalitions have been modified at the presidential levels by Republican surges since 1952 and they controlled the office for sixteen years between 1952 and 1976. (See Table 2 for presidential voting preferences.) The two-party vote for President is shown in Figure 5.

Although the presidential party Democrats began to lose support in the South in 1948, the party has controlled Congress for all but four years since 1932. Stated another way, we are in an era of a comparatively strong Republican presidential coalition and weak congressional party. Although Johnson greatly outdistanced Democratic candidates for the House, Kennedy ran well behind them in 1960. Democratic House candidates collectively polled 7,309,000 more votes than McGovern, and ran 900,000 votes ahead of Carter. Candidates of both parties who run ahead of their own party's presidential nominee are usually incumbents who have built formidable personal machines and performed effective "homework" for their districts. Presidential politics more likely affects congressional districts where there is a competitive two-party system and the lesser candidate may be helped by a popular candidate for President. But in strongly one-party areas, the state and local organizations are frequently able to resist the impact of a presidential swing to the opposite party.

The long-time dominance of one party is a result not only of its ability to adjust its policies to changing needs but also of the fact that new talent tends to join the party that offers the best chance for victory. Patronage, favors, and preferments strengthen the party in power at the local as well as national level. The enduring character of party identification among voters helps the dominant party to remain in control for a long time. On the other hand, the in-party tends to build up resentments and opposition in various quarters, and eventually it is defeated by the opposing party.

NUMBER OF VOTERS, MILLIONS

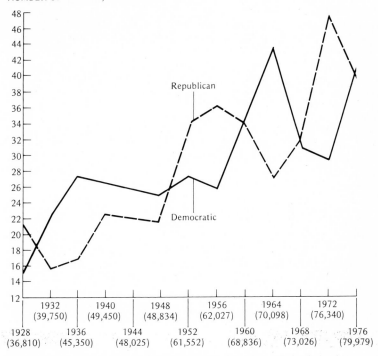

FIGURE 5 The two-party presidential vote, 1928-1976. The number of votes cast for all presidential candidates is given, in millions, below the election dates.

Why two national parties? The two-party system at the national level is attributable in part to the Constitution. The popular election of the President through party slates of electors in each state has a bipolarizing effect. Third-party nominees are rather easily squeezed out. Even the popular Theodore Roosevelt was unable to overcome this handicap in 1912. The single-member congressional district, with selection on the basis of a plurality vote, makes it difficult for a third-party nominee to capture more votes than either of the major-party opponents. A system of proportional representation would be helpful to third parties, and this is a major reason why Republican and Democratic politicians oppose it. Laws regulating party activity in the states also militate against third parties. Major parties receive the political patronage and select the election officers. Petition requirements to place independent or minor-party candidates on the ballot are quite stringent in many states. The division of power between nation and states makes it difficult for a third group to propose an adequate slate for national, state, and local offices. In Canada, it may be noted, minority parties have been able to retain control in a few provinces, but nationally have been unable to challenge the two major parties—the Liberals and Conservatives. In the past, third parties in the United States have arisen, flourished briefly, and then been swallowed up by one of the major parties. Only the Republican party, formed in 1856 when the two old parties were unable to reconcile their internal dissensions over the slavery issue, succeeded in becoming a major party, and the Whig party soon disappeared from the scene.

As noted in Chapter 3, constitutional arrangements are buttressed by social, psychological, economic, and political factors working in favor of a national two-party system. Historically, the nation began with a two-party grouping, and there is a tendency for parties to harden into "ins" and "outs." Practically speaking, third parties have been unable to offer hope of victory to ambitious and competent political talent. Voters are creatures of habit, and tradition has it that voting for a third-party candidate is throwing one's vote away. The strong middle-class character and essential agreement on principle lead the great majority of Americans to take a moderate and center position which has been embraced by Democrats and Republicans.

PARTY SYSTEMS IN THE STATES

Nationally the two parties are loose configurations of local and sectional interests. It is difficult for them to maintain sufficient centralized control and enough ideological agreement to assure a "party line" in Congress. Yet the national party and its leadership have some nationalizing effects, and the local parties function as decentralizers. But national party leaders are reminded daily of the strong centrifugal "states' rights" pull of the parties. They can plead with local party leaders but cannot compel.

Many variations   Americans who think of the United States as operating under a two-party system are often surprised to learn that in about one-half the states one party is dominant in state elections. Schlesinger found a low rate of alternation in the office of governor between 1870 and 1950.[3] More than half the states gave the governorship to one party in 70 percent or more of the elections. Meanwhile, the presidential contests were more competitive than those for governorships.

A large proportion of congressional and state legislative districts are overwhelmingly one-party both inside and outside the South. Even where a state's districts are in overall balance between the parties, many metropolitan districts are heavily Democratic, with small towns and suburban districts consistently Republican. Control of Congress frequently rests in 100 "marginal" districts. Many cities can hardly remember when they had a Republican mayor.

The state party systems vary from strongly dominant one-party to mod-

---

[3]Joseph A. Schlesinger, "A Two-Dimensional Inter-Party Competition," *American Political Science Review*, vol. 49, pp. 1120–1128, 1955.

ified one-party to highly two-party competitive. One analysis found that twenty-three states were genuinely competitive between 1960 and 1974.[4] New York State has a multi-party system, and the major parties must reckon with voting power exercised by the Conservative, Liberal, and sometimes other parties. Since World War II two-party competition has increased in many states, especially for governor and United States senator. Democrats have been more successful for these offices in some Northern states and Republicans in the South. Party loyalties have been fading, and there is greater emphasis in campaigns on the individual candidate. The 1978 election is illustrative of how the dominance of a single party can be broken. Republicans elected a United States senator in Mississippi, a governor in Texas, and swept the governorship and the two United States Senate seats in Minnesota. Meanwhile the Democrats captured the usually Republican governorship in New Hampshire and Kansas.

Some characteristics   Each state's political system has its own peculiar features. A few generalizations may challenge readers to analyze the characteristics and political culture of their own states. As in the nation, there is often a cyclical character to party control, even in two-party states, where the same party may hold the governorship and state legislature for a long period of time. In the modified one-party state, a substantial upheaval is needed for the lesser party to win, and then it may have only a one- or two-term reign before it loses out.

State outcomes are quite insulated from national politics. Prior to Eisenhower, the party carrying the state for the Presidency most often carried the statehouses and frequently the United States Senate seat. In a turnabout the Democrats were very successful during the Eisenhower Administration in capturing and holding a large number of statehouses and legislatures. Despite the huge majorities for Johnson in 1964, the Republicans controlled twenty-six governorships after the 1966 elections. Then, in the face of the Nixon landslide in 1972, the Democrats made huge gains and, with holdovers, held thirty-seven governorships in 1975. Under the same paradoxical pattern, the Republicans made sizable gains with Carter in the White House and in 1979 rebounded from the Nixon-Ford years to hold eighteen governorships and control thirteen state legislatures.

Split-ticket voting is not only limited to statewide-national offices but is found intrastate as well. Numerous states have party splits between the governor and lieutenant governor and the other executive offices. In 1979 seven legislatures had splits between the two houses. Except for a handful of Southern states from 1947 to 1979, every state had an experience with divided government between the governor and legislature. Quite a few had this arrangement for nearly half of the time for the thirty years,

---

[4]For extensive tables and commentary, see Malcolm Jewell and David M. Olson, *American State Political Parties and Elections,* The Dorsey Press, Homewood, Ill., 1978. Books and articles on parties and politics in the individual states are abundant; many are cited in the Jewell-Olson volume.

and prior to 1978 Michigan had the executive and legislative branches in the hands of opposite parties for twenty-four years.[5]

Besides the weakening of party loyalties, other factors contribute to divided government. Gerrymandered districts in some cases lock up many seats for parties and/or incumbents, so they remain less influenced by tides in gubernatorial voting. The use of campaign management firms and media stress the candidate rather than the party label, and other legislative incumbents (similar to Congress) enjoy superiority in campaign funds. Ethnic background, religious affiliation, sectional loyalties, tradition, and the ratio of urban to rural population also affect a state's voting behavior and help cushion local politics from national voting trends for President and Congress.

RATIONALE OF THE TWO PARTIES

American political parties, like their counterparts in other democracies, perform a variety of functions, the emphasis and direction of which vary from community to community. They provide a means of obtaining access to government and for seeking legitimate sanctions to control and direct political power. To this end they propose candidates for public office and conduct elections on their behalf. Once in control of government, they assume responsibility for the direction of the administration of government. Their public officeholders are expected to propose administrative and legislative solutions to public problems. The party out of power is expected to exercise surveillance over the "ins." Through political platforms, speeches by its leaders, press releases and publicity, and activities of its membership, a party performs the role of heightening political interest and of educating its own members and the general electorate.

Supplying personnel   Political recruitment is a prime function of political parties. It is the duty of a party to select its own leaders, find persons to run for public office, and get them elected. Parties also assist in the selection of persons to be appointed to administrative and, sometimes, judicial positions. Party activities in connection with nominating and electing persons to public office are covered in the following chapter.

The function of supplying personnel is accomplished through intricate and decentralized organization. The first is a hierarchy of permanent party committees from precinct to national committee, as shown in Figure 6. The second is the series of conventions that meet every two or four years to adopt platforms, make certain appointments, and vote changes in party rules. Finally, there is amorphous and anomalous additional organizational machinery composed of clubs, auxiliaries, and ad hoc groups whose relationship to the regular party organization is sometimes officially prescribed but more often remains ill-defined. Some of the most powerful persons in the party may neither hold positions in the official organization nor serve as delegates to a party convention.

[5] For a discussion and complete state-by-state table, see *Ibid.*, pp. 253–262.

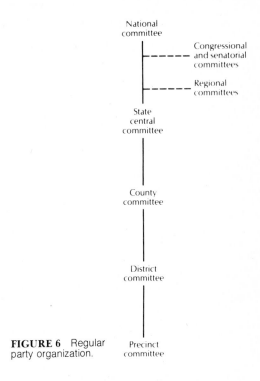

National
committee

Congressional
and senatorial
committees

Regional
committees

State
central
committee

County
committee

District
committee

FIGURE 6 Regular
party organization.

Precinct
committee

Major party organization is predicated on the assumption that it should parallel electoral units. At the base of the organization is the precinct captain, who in some states is popularly elected by voters in his or her precinct. These "cogwheels of democracy," as one writer has described them, are expected to get voters registered and to the polls on Election Day, perform a variety of services for the party, and act as brokers between the voter and government. In many areas, the county committee is composed of the precinct. A ward or legislative-district committee usually serves as an intermediate organization between the precinct and the county committee in the urban areas and is useful in fostering clubs and aiding in state legislative races. In a few states, there is a congressional district organization whose primary function is to conduct the campaign for the election of the party's nominee for Congress and to choose delegates to the national conventions. The county chairperson is a key figure in the party, and the success of the organization is likely to rest upon that individual's personal effectiveness in getting good people to run for the precinct leaders, organizing campaigns, making news for the party, and raising money.

State central committees are concerned with the statewide candidates and elections, raising the state's financial quota, and integrating the work of the county units on behalf of the party. State committees are usually composed of representatives chosen by the county committees. State and county presiding officers are particularly concerned with accommodating factionalism in the interests of the party and its ticket. These individuals may well represent the dominant faction but soon learn the importance of getting support from the other factions.

National party organization is a many-pronged affair.[6] It includes national committees with various youth, womens', ethnic, and diverse other special divisions. Separate policy and campaign committees are found in Congress. Originally the national committee was composed of one man and one woman from each state. In states that elected the Republican presidential candidate or a Republican senator or a majority of its House delegation at the preceding election, the Republican state chairperson serves as a member of the national committee. In a radical reorganization in 1972, the Democrats increased the size of their national committee to 303 members. The national committeeman and woman and the state chairperson and vice-chairperson from each state are automatically on the national committee. The larger states elect additional members, and the committee itself elects twenty-five more members. Three governors and four members of Congress also serve on the committee.[7]

At earlier times the national committees had a large role in directing the presidential campaign. Now they tend to be subordinate to the candidate's committee, such as Nixon's Committee to Re-elect the President. The national committee of the party controlling the White House tends to be an arm of the President, and the committee of the out party serves as the governing body of the national party between elections. From its inception, the national office has been expected to manage the national convention. The committee is the largest single collector, allocator, and spender of the party's financial resources. It conducts research, serves as a source of intelligence, acts as a public relations agent, and has become a symbol of the party's national identity. The national secretariat is a service agency providing state and local organizations with speakers, literature, and information. The national committeemen and committeewomen are channels of communication between the local organization and the national leaders. Both parties have regional associations, such as the Midwest Democratic or Western Republican conferences. These are composed of the national committee members of the various states in these areas. They are used to focus particular attention on the electoral and policy problems of their own section and are regarded as increasingly important, even though they are outside the conventional party hierarchy.

[6]See Hugh A. Bone, *Party Committees and National Politics,* University of Washington Press, Seattle, 1958, and *Political Party Management.* General Learning Corporation, Morristown, N.J., 1973; and Cornelius P. Cotter and Bernard C. Hennessy, *Politics Without Power: The National Party Committees,* Atherton Press, New York, 1964.

[7]The new National Charter adopted in December 1974, added several additional members from the Young Democrats and the Conference of Democratic Mayors. The provisions became effective in 1976 and bring the size of the committee to well over 300. The text of the charter is found in *The New York Times,* Dec. 9, 1974.

Fund raising   The raising of money is a major preoccupation of party committees at all levels.[8] Moreover it is a continuous operation requiring organization and ingenuity. Limitations on spending by a single committee helped to foster much decentralization in the raising and spending of money. A host of nonparty political action committees are engaged in soliciting millions of dollars during campaign years. But only a comparatively small percentage of people give political money.[9] Party and public officeholders and private-group leaders are heavy patrons of fund-raising dinners. Money collected this way generally goes directly into party coffers, but it is not unusual for some of the money to go to candidates rather than into the party treasury. Many donors prefer to give directly to candidates. Party leaders, on the other hand, would rather have money go directly to the official committees, so that they can better allocate needed resources.

Party programs   In their intensely pragmatic approach to politics, party organizations are largely absorbed with recruitment, patronage, and personnel questions. This situation has invited cynics to exaggerate the parties' lack of concern with issues and policies. Parties are interested in those issues that affect the outcome of elections and their control of political power or lack of it. Many party clubs and auxiliary groups give much attention to so-called educational conferences and workshops dealing with issues before the state and nation. They often adopt programs and resolutions and press them on the party's officeholders. For a number of years the national party not controlling the Presidency has created an "advisory" council to issue policy statements—a practice frowned upon by some of the party's congressional representatives, who feel that they should make the record and program of the out party. In 1974 the Democrats called the first midterm national convention. The convention adopted a national charter for the party and recommended an economic program for the members of Congress. Several panels passed along suggestions on several other problems to the Democratic Advisory Council for consideration in preparing the 1976 platform.[10]

Official party statements or platforms are usually adopted biennially by the county and state conventions and at the national level by the presidential nominating conventions every fourth year. Party platforms are criticized as "weasel-worded," very general, and negative, and for failing to show more than negligible differences between Republicans and Democrats. However, citizens will find it worthwhile to analyze several successive national platforms. They will discover, perhaps to their surprise, several differences between the parties in tone, emphasis, and methods, especially in the fields of agriculture, labor, business, social security, and education.

---

[8] Further aspects of party finance are covered in the next chapter.

[9] Thousands of supporters of Goldwater, Wallace, and McGovern, however, were successful in substantially increasing the number of small donors.

[10] For details on this historic convention, see *The New York Times*, Dec. 6-9, 1974.

PARTIES IN GOVERNMENT

Congressional parties Party declarations on public issues have little utility unless they are translated into some party influence on legislation. The model of most parliamentary democracies calls for the "party will" to be reflected through support by the party's members in parliament. American parties seldom get united support from their legislators. Nonetheless, there are several instruments for party influence and leadership in Congress and in most state legislatures. The majority caucus chooses the Speaker of the House and the President *pro tempore* of the Senate. The majority party appoints a patronage chairperson in each house to dispense patronage appointments of the congressional staff. Each party selects a floor leader, whips, and a caucus leader.

The House Republicans formed a broadly representative policy committee in 1949.[11] Until 1973 House Democrats were not successful in establishing a policy committee. That year they created their Steering and Policy Committee, with the Speaker as presiding officer. It was supposed to make recommendations on legislative priorities and policy. In 1975 recommendations for Democratic committee membership and chairpersons was taken from Ways and Means Committee members and placed with the new committee. The latter had a vital part in the "revolution" which deposed several long-time committee chairpersons and subchairpersons. Most of the policy body's suggested changes were upheld in the Democratic caucus.

To some extent the political structure of the House is multifactional rather than the classic two-party model. In 1959 liberal Democrats created the Democratic Study Group (DSG) with elected officers, a whip system, a small staff, a campaign fund-raising unit, and distribution of a weekly newsletter about bills and the parliamentary unit. The DSG also had a prominent role in the changes brought about in early 1975. Parenthetically, the "revolution" shows that an election can have an impact on congressional change. The seventy-five first-term Democrats elected in November 1974 caucused the next month in Washington, D.C., and, among other things, vigorously quizzed committee chairpeople. Then, working with the Steering and Policy Committee and the DSG, they were able to dent the seniority system when the new Congress was organized. Blacks have their own caucus in the House. There is also a Republican Wednesday Club, which is separate from the Republican Policy Committee.

Each party in the House and Senate has a party committee whose function is to help incumbents get reelected and to assist them with certain constituency and personnel problems. Nonincumbents may be helped if these committees feel they have a chance of capturing a seat from the

---

[11] The *Congressional Quarterly Weekly Reports* carry full accounts of party organizational changes in Congress. See also Charles O. Jones, *Party and Policy-Making: The House Republican Policy Committee,* Rutgers University Press, New Brunswick, N.J., 1964; Randall Ripley, *Party Leaders in the House of Representatives,* The Brookings Institution, Washington, D.C., 1967, and *Majority Party Leadership,* Little, Brown and Company, Boston, 1968; and Robert L. Peabody, *Leadership in Congress: Stability, Succession, and Change,* Little, Brown and Company, Boston, 1976.

opposition. These congressional campaign committees, like the national committees, raise and dispense money, conduct research, and prepare roll call votes and studies. Each party in the Senate has a "policy committee" supported by public funds. They likewise have research staffs and issue strongly partisan statements but do not duplicate the activities of the regular party committees. The policy committees concern themselves with legislative agendas and the reconciliation of factionalism and issue position statements only on issues about which the party is united. They serve as an arm of the party leadership in Congress and proclaim the legislative record of their party.

The standing-committee chairpersons and the ranking minority members of committees enjoy their positions quite largely by reason of seniority. The chairpersons do not function as a collegial body, but their power limits, to some extent, that of the speaker and floor leaders and assumes the dispersion of power and leadership in Congress. At the same time the majority floor leader's position is one of great influence, and he frequently behaves as if he were a trustee of the party's record. Party pressures are but one of many influences on a member of Congress. The attitudes of constituents, organized interest groups, the state delegation in Congress, and personal friendships in and out of Congress are often more influential than party label on crucial votes.

Scholars have analyzed roll call votes on policy questions as one way of ascertaining divergencies between Democrats and Republicans. Table 6 lists party unity votes and several votes on important policy measures. In the years selected we note that the percentage of time a majority of Democrats voted opposite a majority of Republicans varied from twenty-seven to forty-five. House and Senate Republicans had badly divided ranks on federal aid to education, Medicare, and the 1970 Civil Rights Act. Members of both houses agreed on funding the supersonic transport. As one reviews these and a great many other roll call votes, it is clear that although *all* Republicans and *all* Democrats do not vote the same, there is quite often a tendency for *most* Republicans to vote in opposition to *most* Democrats on controversial issues. Democrats are readier to support federal interventions than Republicans, and are more prolabor, while Republicans are more probusiness. Party labels in Congress and in the more competitive state legislatures do have some validity. The major parties serve as vehicles of competition for office and for aggregating and compromising interests.

Executive parties   The American major parties are, electorally speaking, executive centered. There is larger voter turnout when executives are on the ballot than during the midterm congressional and state legislative elections. The President and most governors are regarded as the leaders of their parties. The executive becomes the symbol of the party. Studies of voter perceptions suggest a close identity between the image of the candidate and the image of the party. Yet as we have seen, voting tends to be two- or three-tiered. Persons may vote for a Republican President but support Democratic candidates for Congress and the state legislature. As chief legislators, executives formulate programs—partly in con-

TABLE 6 Party voting in congress

I. *Party Unity**

| Year | Percent of Party Unity Roll Calls | |
	Senate	*House*
1964	36	49
1968	32	35
1972	36	27
1976	37	36
1978	45	33

II. *Selected Roll Calls*

| Measure | House | | Senate | |
	Yea	*Nay*	*Yea*	*Nay*
Aid to elementary-secondary education (1965)	228	57 D	55	4 D
	35	96 R	18	14 R
Medicare (1965)	237	48 D	57	7 D
	70	68 R	13	17 R
Civil Rights Act (1970)	152	89 D	42	17 D
	77	106 R	29	3 R
Appropriations for supersonic transport (1971)	114	132 D	19	34 D
	90	60 R	27	17 R

*Party Unity means the percent of recorded votes that split the parties, with a majority of voting Democrats opposing a majority of voting Republicans.
Source: The *Congressional Quarterly Weekly Reports,* from which these figures were adopted, provide a summary of party divisions on the main roll calls each week.

formance with the party platform and partly not. In essence the executive's policies are broadly conceived as the party's policies.

The executive party extends beyond the person and his or her staff to include the cabinet and a considerable number of positions exempt from the civil service. These officials often appear as partisan functionaries, speaking for the administration's program and aiding in reelection campaigns. The respective state and national committees are largely dominated by the incumbent executives and are expected to remain loyal to the chief.

Presidents Nixon, Ford, and Carter often had trouble mobilizing the votes of their own partisans in Congress. Members of Congress often are elected without benefit of presidential coattails and frequently run ahead of the President in their own districts. Members of Congress in most cases receive minimal financial help from the party organization in their campaigns. Therefore neither the President nor the party organization has much electorally derived leverage over their own members of Congress in terms of presidential programs.

The President looks to others for support. The press conference, television and other appearances, and messages to Congress are a means of rallying public support which may not be regularly ignored by legislators. The executive also elicits the support of leaders of powerful interest groups, party leaders, governors, mayors, and so on, who in turn may place pressure on those in Congress. Administrative officials spend much time in working with special clienteles to persuade recalcitrant lawmakers to back executive requests.

Presidents have Capitol Hill liaison persons who deal individually with lawmakers for support. Some patronage exists, as well as support or lack of support for pet projects in a lawmaker's district. A member of Congress who wants a certain appointment in his or her district or perhaps a public works project may discover that support for them requires a vote supporting the President. Congressional leaders are regularly invited to the White House to discuss programs and strategy. Social invitations to White House affairs may be used to buttress friendships, which in turn may be converted into payoffs on legislation.

The fact that the President (or governor) prepares the budget is important to legislators because they would like to get their measures included. Conversely, the budget director or some other executive official may make clear that a pet bill of a member of Congress will be subject to a veto. The veto, or the threat of a veto, can be a powerful tool in protecting the President's program, which he may label as the party program. In sum there is an important executive-legislative relationship. The President has significant formal and informal powers to obtain congressional support. The use of the "party" label is one part of this arsenal, and some Presidents have been skilled in the use of it. At the same time the late seventies were a time of much congressional independence both of the executive and the party label. This made it difficult to obtain consensus in many areas—especially energy, inflation, and some areas of foreign policy.

Party government   Party government is a method of implementing majority rule, ideally with each party presenting a set of coherent policy alternatives. The party's candidates commit themselves to the program and assume collective responsibility for enacting it. A measure of party discipline within the legislative party is necessary to this end.

Since the 1890s there has been a normative argument over the "adequacy" of the two-party system, a debate provocative of a rash of literature since the appearance of a report by a group of political scientists calling for more "responsible" parties.[12] There is disagreement and vague-

---

[12] *Toward a More Responsible Two-Party System,* published as a supplement to the *American Science Review,* vol. 44, September 1950. For overall discussion and bibliography, see Austin Ranney, *The Doctrine of Responsible Party Government: Its Origin and Present State,* University of Illinois Press, Urbana, Ill., 1962. See also James M. Burns, *The Deadlock of Democracy,* Prentice-Hall, Inc., Englewood Cliffs, N.J., 1963, and E. E. Schattschneider, *Party Government,* Holt, Rinehart and Winston, New York, 1962. It should be noted that within Congress there is party discipline on matters of organization. Reform Democrats in the 1975 Democratic "revolution" also evaluated committee chairpersons and appropriations subcommittee chairpersons in terms of their previous party support record.

ness over the meaning of adequacy. Adequacy in terms of supplying voters with choices of persons for public office? Control of public leaders? Offering alternative policies? Assuming responsibility for policies when in control of government? Coalition building of aggregates of voters and interests? Educating the public in issues?

To a considerable extent the differences over party role are matters of what the parties *are* doing as compared to what some think they *ought* to be doing. It is also a question of whether one sees the two major parties as shaped by the political environment or believes in the capacity and desirability of the parties to shape the political environment. Defenders of the present system see the parties as only one mechanism in the overall political system, as largely what they are because of the system. To change parties in the direction of centralization and ideological consensus on policy alternatives, so runs the argument, is to invite a chain reaction in the political system which might well lead to instability and exacerbate conflict. Parties currently fit in with the dispersion of power. Critics of the party system deny that instability would result from greater cohesion on policy, and stress the need for public policies to meet the great changes taking place in society.

Proposals for stronger and better-disciplined parties have received little public support. The majority of citizens prefer the present system, in which the representative's duty is to satisfy constituents rather than the national party leaders. For the present, the majority of those concerned with American politics believe the existing party system superior to a more centralized one in terms of stability, consensus, and compromise. They see parties as articulating and promoting democratic values and offering a mechanism for political participation and processes. In contrast to interest groups, the major parties moderate and embrace a wide range of interests. There remains in the nation a sharp division of opinion over what parties really *can* and *should* do.

MINOR PARTIES

Nearly all the voting studies since 1940 have given little attention to minor parties because their numbers have been small. Although third-party presidential candidates occasionally poll a substantial vote (5.4 percent in 1948 and 14 percent in 1968), most of their voters tend to return to one of the major parties at the next election. In a few states and cities, third parties—Progressives, Socialists, and Farmer-Laborites—have won legislative seats, governorships, and mayoralty offices. It is highly probable, however, that voter attachment in such cases was to candidates rather than to the party. The large vote polled by Theodore Roosevelt's Progressive party in 1912 and Robert M. La Follette's bid for the Presidency in 1924 was a result of their personal followings and prior identification as Republicans rather than support of the new party. Both were aided by a schism in the Republican party. In each case the new party quickly folded, and its voters returned to their former parties at the next election.

Third parties are movements of protest against the old parties and government policies in time of crisis or depression. Only one third party in the history of the country—the Republican party—succeeded in becoming one of the two major parties, because of the disappearance of the Whig party when it was unable to unite on the issue of slavery. The hard times on the farms in the latter half of the nineteenth century witnessed the rise of the Populist party in the Middle West and the South, but like other third-party movements, it declined when times became better, and its proposed reforms were adopted by one of the major parties. The Socialist party sought at the turn of the century to capitalize on labor and agrarian unrest to build an ideological party, but after 1912 it declined in strength.

In addition to third parties based upon major-party secession and schism and upon an ideology such as socialism, third parties have arisen around a single issue, such as antislavery or prohibition. Very small right-wing parties have appeared on the ballot in some states since World War II. These attract only an infinitesimal number of adherents. In 1968, however, former Alabama Governor George Wallace led a formidable third-party movement on issues favoring "law and order" and opposing federal intervention, doctrines that had special appeal to some conservatives and those anxious about black militancy. Many supporting the Southern-based "states' rights" third parties of 1948 and 1968 hoped to capture enough electoral votes to throw the election of the President into the House of Representatives.

Dissonant minorities of blacks, Chicanos, laborers, agrarians, and peace advocates have experimented with minor parties as a channel for getting their messages to the public, but with little hope for electoral success. Proselytizing the cause itself seems better served through non-party mass movements using such tactics as demonstrations, boycotts, strikes, and conventional lobbying tactics with public officals. Doctrinaire socialist groups, such as the Socialist Workers, Socialist Labor, and Communists, continue to put money and effort into fielding candidates for the Presidency and some other offices.[13]

POLITICAL LEADERSHIP

Leadership takes many forms, though all leadership is based upon a relationship between leader and followers. Followers must see their leader as performing a role that takes them toward shared objectives. A leadership situation may include both formal authority and informal influence, and the leader becomes more or less the focal point for the activity of the group.

Party leadership   Party leadership is provided by thousands of precinct captains, committee members, county, district, state, and national chair-

[13]Laws in many states make it difficult for minor parties to qualify their candidates for the ballot. In addition to books on specific minor parties, two general works are W. B. Hesseltine, *Third Party Movements in the United States,* Van Nostrand Reinhold Company, New York, 1962, and Daniel A. Mazmanian, *Third Parties in Presidential Elections,* The Brookings Institution, Washington, D.C., 1974.

persons, and elective and appointive public officers. Despite the hierarchy of party committees shown in Figure 6, there is no chain of command, and each level of leaders is essentially independent from others. This gives great autonomy to the functionaries. A national chairperson or committee member cannot compel the thousands of state and county chairpersons to operate to the national leader's liking. Most precinct committee chairpersons are popularly elected and cannot be removed or effectively disciplined by these county officials.

What kinds of persons become the party's leaders and activists? Are they representative of the party's rank-and-file voters? Studies of local party functionaries show enough diversity to defy generalization. Occupationally, county chairpersons show large numbers from the fields of law, farming, and business management. Few come from the ranks of teachers, manual laborers, and sales-clerical personnel. A majority served apprenticeships as precinct or district leaders and have been in politics a long time.

Up to World War II precinct leaders in the big-city organizations tended to come from the lower classes and were often on the city payroll. Currently many more college-educated people have become activists, and more seem to be ideologically oriented than formerly. The higher party leaders, such as county chairpersons and national convention delegates, also are more ideologically oriented than the rank-and-file voters. Many more young people appear to be seeking precinct positions than formerly. Party rules generally require the chairperson and vice-chairperson to be of opposite sexes, and some precincts also have two positions which are divided between the sexes. In general, precinct leaders tend to belong to the dominant ethnic, economic, and religious groups in their district, thereby reflecting the values and prejudices of their neighborhoods.

What motivates persons to enter party politics? In earlier days economic incentives were important—one obtained a job with the government or obtained economic preferment. The incentive system today embraces many motives. A group of "amateur democrats" have entered both parties with a strong interest in promoting specific public policies or influencing and changing priorities. Some hope to become national convention delegates or to be associated with a particular campaign. Others are motivated by hoped-for excitement and social associations. There is, therefore, a complicated incentive system of psychic, social, tangible, and intangible satisfactions from becoming "part of the action."

Function   Presidential leadership is providing the subject of an increasing number of books and articles. The misdeeds of the Nixon White House focused attention on "presidential style," and the growth of what some called the "imperial Presidency," Particular attention is given to the huge institutionalization and specialization in the office of the Presidency and a swelling of the staff. Governors of the larger states similarly have numerous assistants to aid them in their leadership functions. Ultimately, however, elected executives must assume responsibility for the actions and decisions of the specialized corps surrounding them. They must carefully select and manage these staffs. Leaders must see that their staffs do not unduly isolate them from constituents or impair their representative functions.

Whether the leadership position is institutionalized or not, the task of the public figure is exacting. Politicians believe in the art of the possible. It is their job to find solutions and compromises that may not please everyone but are nonetheless acceptable and durable. Those in the lower-echelon leadership positions perform the chores of the public's housekeeping that are ignored by most citizens. American legislators, much more than their foreign counterparts, are expected to be servants for their constituents.

As representatives and symbols of their districts, states, or nations, it is the function of the public figures to articulate their problems, goals, and aspirations. They suggest proposals and make decisions on what is to be done and who is to get what. They are the voters' alter ego and reflect the temper of the times. In turn, they interpret government to those whom they represent, a function of education.

Qualities   It is a favorite sport to speculate on the motivations of leaders and whether a potential candidate "has what it takes" to be a leader. A long list of traits that appear conducive to leadership has been compiled by psychologists and social scientists. Versatility, imagination, force of will, high oratorical competence, showmanship, intuition, and flexibility are but a few of the attributes allegedly necessary in politics.

The possession of certain of these personality traits is undoubtedly useful, both in getting elected and in performing successfully in a position of leadership. But these traits are not the only, or perhaps the most important, aspect of leadership. Politics is not an exact science, and we cannot say precisely what qualities are necessary for satisfactory leadership. Leadership is a relationship to a specific situation. The "great engineer" abilities of Herbert Hoover appealed to voters in 1928, but with a radically changed situation in 1932 a far different type of leader was desired. One might make a fine governor of Pennsylvania but be a disappointment as a United States senator because of a significant difference between the roles of the two positions. An extraordinarily competent state party chairperson might well be a mediocre governor because of a different group involvement of the two positions.

The American political system affords an untold number of leadership opportunities in all sorts of community, civic, business, occupational, religious, ethnic, and other groups, as well as in official and party organizations, for ours is a truly pluralistic society. Skills in leadership may be developed in many different types of organizations—the PTA, the League of Women Voters, a labor or business organization, as well as party organizations.

NONPARTISAN POLITICS

Widespread use   Many popular officeholders cultivate the image of being above party and appeal, in nonpartisan terms, for the support of members of all parties. Nonpartisan elections are provided by law in many American communities. In the overwhelming majority of cities with commission and city-manager forms of government, and in 40 percent of the mayor-council cities, nonpartisan elections are used for the election of council members. Though no tally has been made, it is probable that half of the elective public offices are filled by nonpartisan ballot. The rationale for nonpartisan local elections, which spread widely during the early decades of the twentieth century to many cities, schools, and other local bodies, was that local affairs should be divorced from national and state politics. It was argued that partisan politics must be "kept out" of schools, health departments, and so on.

Effects   Many questions are asked about the results of nonpartisan elections. Are they really nonpartisan? Have they enabled small groups to control local governments? Have they hurt Democratic and Republican organizations and benefited one party over another? Experience is so diverse that by selecting one city over another one might find "proof" to answer these questions according to one's own predilection. As for their influence on parties, the system certainly has removed certain amounts of patronage from the local organizations. Adrian concludes that, with few exceptions, "nonpartisan elections have accomplished what they set out to do. They have effectively removed the regular party machinery from involvement in certain kinds of local, judicial and state elections."[14] Although nonpartisan elections did not "ruin" the parties, they required them to work out a modus vivendi with the system. Party organizations usually officially remain neutral in the elections, but party leaders may and often do participate individually and through nonparty groups.

The significant thing about nonpartisan elections is that politics is not adjourned or eliminated but, on the contrary, that a different form of politics replaces the older partisan style. Nonpartisan government requires politicians, for politics is the art of governance. Different groups may become involved in local nonpartisan elections, and the relative degree of involvement of other groups may differ markedly from that in a partisan congressional or state election. In California nonpartisan elections, the most influential groups were found to be, in order of influence, newspapers, merchants, service clubs, and women's organizations; and labor unions are of relatively small significance.[15] In the same state, large numbers of business and professional persons who have experience in civic and advisory bodies, many acquaintances, and large personal followings are winners of the local offices. These factors plus newspaper influences (usually Republican) undoubtedly contribute to the success in local elections of a sizable preponderance of registered Republicans. Many nonpartisan positions are part-time and are compatible with business and professional occupations, whereas workers may find their workday less

[14] Charles Adrian, "A Typology for Nonpartisan Elections," *Western Political Quarterly,* vol. 12, p. 458, June 1959. See also Charles Adrian, *Governing Our Fifty States and Their Communities,* 2d ed., McGraw-Hill Book Company, New York, 1967.

[15] Eugene Lee, *The Politics of Nonpartisanship,* University of California Press, Berkeley, Calif., 1960.

flexible for building support and also for holding office, if successful. Elections tend also to be run on the basis of personal qualifications of the candidates rather than on issues, a politics of personal acquaintance. In nonpartisan politics a person without formal party backing must appeal for the broadest possible support; though not beholden to a party organization for nomination and election, the "unbossed" person may be bossed by others who engineered his or her venture into public office.

The side-by-side existence of partisan and nonpartisan politics in many American communities is further illustration of the fractionated, decentralized American political system. Party organizations are still essential in the gigantic effort involved in the winning of the numerous partisan offices. Nonpartisan politics undoubtedly encourages many competent men and women to seek public office who would not do so if they had to run as Democrats or Republicans. There is much to be said for both types of recruitment for public office, and pragmatic Americans have avowed, in many American municipalities, that they want both.

THE PARTY SYSTEM UNDER STRESS

The problems of a troubled society in the eighties are troubling party leaders. Polls show a massive disenchantment with, if not distrust of, the political parties as well as most other private and public institutions. The public's ambivalence about political parties and low level of support for them was present even before the traumas of Watergate and Vietnam. A Harris poll in September 1976 showed that, by a 54 to 31 percent majority, divided party control between the President and Congress was seen as a "good way to be sure that one party can't get away with corruption and misuse of power in office." Some see a new politics, without parties, on the way. Others say that the system as we have known it for over a century is dead though not yet interred.

Irrespective of the validity of these gloomy views, there is a malaise, and parties cannot hope to monopolize politics as they once did. Many forces dating back at least a generation have combined with new stresses to place great strain on the party system.

Since the 1930s the importance of technology in campaigns and in politics has grown. Public relations and advertising firms were hired to "package" candidates, and this included fund-raising and campaign strategies. Candidates were often urged to play down, if not ignore, party labels. For the more important offices, television became a major source of information about candidates (and events), and what was seen on the screen became "reality" for the voter. Voters were in a position to act on what they saw, not what party activists told them. The latter were more and more bypassed, both as money raisers and as campaigners, in favor of electronic media. As will be seen in the next chapter, the rise of separate political-action committees has also preempted much of the work formerly performed by precinct and other party workers. Where officeholders and candidates used to rely heavily on party functionaries for intelligence, they now look more and more to what computerized public opinion polls tell them. Succinctly, the new technology has reduced the mediatorial function of parties.

Up to this point we have noted several times the decline in voter turn-out and the increase in split-ticket voting. Beginning in the 1950s it became apparent that party labels were less of a cue-giving device, with a con-comitant decline in casting straight-ticket ballots. Personality politics encouraged emphasis on the image and the perceived qualities of the individual. As noted before, the decline of patronage and preferment incen-tives has forced party chairpersons to find new motivations to use when recruiting party workers. In the 1960s a better-educated stream of persons were moving into party organizations, seeing them as agents of change. Some left shortly in disillusionment because parties were not effective in initiating the kinds of changes they desired. Many of these new "amateurs" were ideologically oriented but found that the major parties were much less ideological than they hoped. This was true of many rightists who sought to use the Republicans to elect Goldwater in 1964 and of liberal-leftists in the McGovern movement in 1972. There are still many "ama-teurs" in both parties, but numerous ideologues moved into nonparty organizations.

The 1970s saw the rise of single-issue politics. Many of the groups con-cerned with such issues were very well financed, and often their tactics were highly emotional because the issues possessed religious and moral overtones. Often these were negative or "anti," such as abortion, rights for homosexuals, emancipation for certain groups, busing to achieve racial integration, amnesty for Vietnam objectors, and decriminalization of mari-juana. Other groups fought for restoration of prayer in the public schools. A nonreligious issue arousing great emotion was opposition to gun con-trol. Opposite organizations arose to counter these. Both sides pressured parties to adopt platform planks and to commit candidates to uncompro-mising stands. These issues have become deeply disturbing to the polity.

Two aspects of the new single-issue politics are to be noted. First, it is not novel. One can point to the abolition of slavery and the prohibition of alcoholic beverages as great emotional issues of yesteryear. The current problem is that many more issues of this kind are appearing today, and they have become of high salience, attracting much money and energy. Second, it is difficult for a party system based on coalition politics to ac-commodate many of these interests because the latter are uncompromis-ing in their stands. The issues cross party lines. The party leaders tend to be pragmatic on divisive issues and do not wish to take a stand that may cost votes among those who insist on purity on the one issue as the price of support.

Another development in the 1960s and 1970s was a new emphasis on "open" government. For private groups this involved better representa-tion in the decision-making bodies of bar, medical, and most other groups, as well as in the political party's organization. Several party organizations underwent structural changes. Students in many colleges obtained mem-bership on academic committees and boards of regents. Public-agency and private-group meetings were expected to be open to the public, and executive sessions were suspect. Nearly every state, some through the initiative process, adopted legislation which would provide public disclosure of political finance and often of the financial assets of candidates. Lobbyists came under more strict regulation and were required to disclose more information on their activities, especially finance. Many states wrote new regulations for campaign finance. Congress moved in the direction of substantial public financing of presidential elections (see the next chapter). As if these changes were not enough, since 1968 the process of selecting delegates to national conventions, and the operation of the conventions, has undergone the greatest revision since 1832. (This too is reviewed in the following chapter.)

The accumulation of these changes and emphases can be regarded as revolutionary in impact, or nearly so. Parties have always been slow to change, and it is difficult for them to keep pace with these movements and developments, which are eroding the old-style politics. Watergate and the resignation of President Nixon brought new problems for Republicans, as the struggle between the regulars and the former McGovern supporters has for the Democrats. Few decades in history have seen as many new forces and stresses placed upon the major parties as was witnessed in the seventies.

Does this mean the demise of the two-party system, such as occurred for a time after 1816? Not likely. Rather, what is being witnessed is a decline rather than a demise. Parties are no longer dominant—nor can they hope to be—in nominations and elections. But they are still important and influential in these processes. The party still lends the legitimacy of a label to those seeking state and national office and for organizing legislatures. Notwithstanding the Nixon Presidency, the Chief Executive is still at the head of an executive-led party. Out parties will continue to provide opposition for the ins. Both parties still compete for public office. The fact remains, also, that millions of Americans still retain a strong party loyalty and cast a straight-ticket ballot. Millions of others retain a modicum of party identification, and the label is a reference for them.

The parties are adjusting to demands for change. The Democrats radically altered their national committee and convention structure and rules and held the first biennial national convention in 1974. In a first for both parties, women were chosen to lead their national committees in the seventies. The mass party still offers a channel for persons of lesser status and power to participate in politics and for some an opportunity to attain a party or public office.

It seems unlikely that parties can perform the function of integration and aggregation of interests to the same extent as formerly. There are new, highly divisive interests, programs, and ideologies which no one party can hope to manage, given the realities of pragmatic politics. Fragmented politics seems here to stay. The parties are more controlled by their environment than they are able to control it. They can modify their surrounding political culture only a finite amount. The extent to which the parties can contribute to change or prevent it remains a moot point and causes tensions between and within the organizational and government wings of the party.

Alignments are likely to remain fluid in the 1980s even though Carter was able to restore the older Democratic coalition enough to be elected in 1976. Painful problems especially in energy and inflation, plagued the

Carter administration, and in the summer of 1979 the President himself received an all-time low rating for Presidents in the polls. The three presidential elections in the eighties will see the emergence of new leaders in both parties. Each party will try to rally its hard-core clientele and seek new supporters, especially among young adults. Presidents face the problem of influencing a highly independent Congress and of being strong and effective in seeking public support for the allocation of resources, which are less abundant than formerly. As in the past, the major parties will continue to be related to the development of social, economic, and political democracy. As democratic processes mature and change and new interests arise, parties must adjust to survive. In the present state of a highly complex set of pluralistic interests and organizations, parties cannot expect to dominate the people's loyalties and interests and supply the major instrument to bring about political change. If these are the expectations of the major parties, frustration and failure seem assured.

REVIEW QUESTIONS

1 In the perspective of party history, what inferences and generalizations can you make about the development of American parties, alternation in power, and alignments and cleavages?

2 At the present time what do you regard as the differences between Democrats and Republicans? State your criteria and defend them.

3 *(a)* Select one or two states that have "divided government" and try to find out the reasons for it. *(b)* Is better government assured by placing control of the executive and legislative branches in the hands of the same political party? Substantiate your answer.

4 What inducements other than patronage can be offered to recruit local party workers? Are the modern electronic and other media likely to replace both the old-style bosses and new-style leaders? Why or why not?

5 Under what circumstances might the minor-party vote for President rise to 5 percent or more?

6 Many mayors and city council members are elected on a nonpartisan ballot. Would it be desirable to elect members of state legislatures and Congress in the same manner? Why or why not?

7 Select a few party officials and find out *(a)* how they became interested in party politics, and *(b)* how and why they became party leaders.

8 How are your local party leaders trying to meet the current stresses and problems? To what extent have their efforts been successful?

9 What are the advantages and disadvantages of the use of the initiative process to permit voter enactment of public policy?

5 NOMINATIONS AND ELECTIONS

In this chapter the familiar refrain of decentralization and pluralism is heard again. It now reappears in the nominating and electoral processes. In the early days of the United States, candidates were named by an inner circle of party leaders. Members of the state legislature met in a party caucus to designate nominees for state offices. Because of the objections to the undemocratic character of the caucus, it was superseded by the party nominating convention. During the present century the more complex and decentralized direct primary was substituted for the convention.

NOMINATIONS IN THE STATES

Conventions   The convention system that replaced the early party caucus permitted a large number of active party members to take part in nominations without depriving the party organization of the historic function of selection of candidates. But the convention fell into disrepute because of too-frequent domination by undesirable factions, machines, and underworld elements. Some conventions were packed by party bosses, and party voters failed to respond to their new opportunity to vote for delegates to conventions. As early as 1842, the Democratic organization in Crawford County, Pennsylvania, instituted a voluntary primary system under which the voters of the party chose the nominees, but it was not until 1907 that a mandatory direct primary system was adopted in Wisconsin. Now all fifty states use the primary system for nominating some or all state and local candidates.

The convention system is today employed in a very few states to select certain candidates for statewide offices. Party conventions are still used to select some delegates to national conventions, party officials, and to serve as a forum for would-be nominees. County and state conventions often adopt party platforms that hopefully, but seldom, bind nominees to policy positions. Conventions are usually arenas for factional struggles.

Direct primaries   Primaries took the power of selection away from a corps of leaders and activists and placed it by law in the hands of the voters, thus further democratizing the nominating process but weakening party control over nominations. Primaries raise many problems for the candidate, the party organization, the state legislature, and the voters. For the aspirants, the primary requires them to wage a campaign before the primary election to win nomination, and if they win, to conduct a second campaign before the general election. This is likely to require much energy and money. Candidates, moreover, must conduct their campaign so as not to foreclose party aid in the general election. Party organizations in some states are forbidden by law to endorse a nominee in a primary, and in other areas a strong tradition of neutrality exists. Because the aspirants may win nomination on their own and subsequently win the election, they may be uncooperative with organization leaders on patronage and deviate from the general policy positions of the party. As such the primary may be a divisive factor within a party. Primaries impose the extra burden on the voter of making wise choices among the many candidates in the primary election. Public authorities have the job of legislating the type of primary and how it will be administered.

A major question for legislative determination is who should be permitted to vote in the party primary and what tests of party membership should be applied. Primary laws show great variation but fall broadly into four categories: closed, open, blanket, and nonpartisan. The last-mentioned is used before nonpartisan elections. In a few communities using the nonpartisan primary, a nominee polling more than 50 percent of the primary vote is declared elected; a more common practice is for the two highest candidates to run in the final election. Without the guidance of party labels and with the lessened clarity of nonpartisan politics, voters must base their choices on other factors, with the result that turnout is likely to be low. Voting in the closed primary is possible only for persons who register as partisans or who openly declare their party affiliation at the polls. This is the most widely used form. In the open primary, which is used in a dozen states, registered voters may vote in the primary of either party without registering as partisans or announcing their party affiliation at the polls, but they may vote only for the candidates of one party. The blanket primary system, used in Alaska and Washington, does not limit voters to the candidates of one party but permits them to vote for the candidates of their choice, irrespective of party.

Preference for one type of primary over another depends on one's outlook on the role of the party. Most party leaders favor the closed primary on the ground that persons unwilling to register their affiliation have no claim to participate in the choice of party nominees. The open primary, moreover, weakens the party identification of the voter. Party regulars see the closed primary as promoting greater party responsibility and helping them to keep mavericks and independents from winning the party's nominations. They also oppose the open primary because it permits voters of one party to vote in the primary of the opposite party, which they may be inclined to do if there is no contest in their own party.

Advocates of the open primary contend that voters should not be required to register as partisans or to announce their party affiliation, which is contrary to the principle of the secrecy of the ballot, and that the danger of party voters crossing over (raiding) in the primary is relatively small. They also contend that independents who decline to register as partisans should not be deprived of the vote in the primary election, which is usually more important than the final election. The blanket type of primary, which is used in Washington, permits the voter a free choice of any candidate irrespective of party. It has worked reasonably well in that state, resulting in vigorous contests and a strong two-party system.

Party influences   Parties have a key function in recruiting, screening, and promoting candidates for elective office. Under caucus and convention systems of nomination, candidates selected by the party leaders were, as a rule, strong partisans who were willing to follow party leadership—attributes not necessarily possessed by candidates who win the primary nomination in primary elections. Nevertheless, the direct primary has by no means removed the party leaders from the nominating process. Control varies from formal slate making to important but invisible influence. In some large cities, such as Chicago, New York, and Philadelphia, county leaders regularly present a slate, making it difficult to challenge the organization ticket. Where the county chairpersons are officially neutral, many of the rank-and-file workers back candidates; thus the primaries afford a method of choosing among factions.

There is, of course, much informal consultation before the primary, and party leaders often seek out suitable candidates to run in the primaries. Leaders usually want to avoid primary fights that may stir up internal strife. It is not unusual for party leaders to discourage certain aspirants from entering the primary because of the danger to "party unity" or because of the formidable obstacles to finding financial and other support.

In several states, slate making is formalized by law, whereby the organization may endorse candidates through a preprimary convention. Candidates must receive a certain number of votes at the convention in order to receive official designation on the ballot. This may permit two or more persons to obtain endorsement. Gradually, candidates have found it advantageous to receive official approval.

In California, endorsement is made by unofficial or extralegal organizations known as the California Republican Assembly and California Democratic Council. These groups go beyond endorsement to supply help in the primary campaign. Very few major candidates have successfully opposed their choices, and there is a tendency for persons to bow out of the race if they fail to obtain the endorsement. Although the California organizations are outside of the regular party machinery, their close identification with the party leadership gives them a semiofficial status in the public mind.

Popular control?   Party leaders must reckon with the fact that the approval of the party's members will be needed in order to win the primary. Contested primaries are often factional struggles between those having the support of most of the organization and those who in one degree or another are antiorganization. A number of contests are simply personal, and each candidate builds his or her own support from allied groups and gathers help from certain of those in the hierarchy. Many are reasonably visible liberal-conservative cleavages and give the party voter some choice of approach as well as of personality. In one-party areas the primary frequently affords the only meaningful election because of negligible opposition in the general election. Nomination results from much informal bargaining among party and interest-group leaders and factions. In some Southern states, intraparty alliances are durable enough to continue from primary to primary and, on the surface at least, bear some resemblance to a two-party struggle. Because of the importance of the Southern Democratic primaries, a runoff is usually held between the two leading candidates if neither receives a majority.

In a convention system or where the leaders draw up the slate, there is balancing of the ticket in terms of the big cities and "outstate," various factions, and perhaps among the large ethnic and religious minorities. Such "rational" choices are possible when decisions are made in a smoke-filled room. In the direct primary, decisions are made by a majority or plurality of votes, with possible anomalous results of "unbalance." In such cases, the party voters may propose a slate of candidates weaker in terms of general election voting appeal than would have been presented by the hierarchy.

Non-Southern primaries, as noted in Chapter 3, have failed to attract consistently high voter participation, and it is doubtful that the participants represent an accurate or broad cross-section of the party. Even in those Southern areas where the primary election is more significant than the general election, primaries do not invariably attract large voter turnout. In other states, a 50 percent vote of registered voters in the primary is exceptional, and in many primaries the vote drops as low as 30 percent. There is little, if any, difference in the percentage of vote cast in open and closed primary states, which indicates that the form of the primary election is not the determining factor in the size of the vote.

As with many other opportunities for political involvement, large numbers of voters fail to participate in the nominating process. The selection is influenced by such factors as incumbency, attractiveness of personality, group support and alliances, and available campaign funds.

Congressional nominations   Nominations for Congress provide another illustration of decentralized politics. Candidates for President and Vice President are designated in a national convention, whereas nomination of their party's lawmakers takes place in hundreds of primaries and conventions. There is a strong tendency to nominate and reelect incumbent representatives and senators irrespective of their party loyalty, if they have guarded the interest of their states or districts. The candidate need not be *persona grata* to the presidential nominee. President Franklin D. Roosevelt spoke against certain incumbents in the 1938 Democratic primaries but won very few battles and incurred much criticism. Primaries are often fought out along ideological lines, but the national party leaders, including the President, are expected to remain neutral. As noted in the previous chapter, voters frequently separate presidential and congressional elections in their minds. The local responsibility for nominating persons to Congress emphasizes parochial interests and tends to diminish rather than strengthen the national party. The national party is, in effect, deprived of a critical mechanism for improving party discipline. Members of Congress are often not integrated into the structure of local party organizations. Each tends to develop his or her own personal organization to assure nomination and election.

PRESIDENTIAL NOMINATIONS

The national convention is one of the most colorful political shows on earth and is carried to the world via radio, television, and film. No other nation nominates its Chief Executive in such a manner. In addition the convention adopts the national party platform and acts as the sovereign body for the national party. This unique institution has grown up outside the Constitution and is unregulated by Congress. Congress, however, makes appropriations to both political parties to help defray convention costs.

The national committees set the time and place of the national conventions and allot the number of votes to each state. Apportionment of votes and rules for selecting delegates have undergone radical change since 1960.[1] Both parties have reacted to pressures to make their conventions more "representative" by increasing the number of delegates. In 1980 respective scheduled sizes were 3,331 for the Democrats and 1,993 for the Republicans. Each party uses a different formula for allocation of delegates to states, but distribution is accorded first on the number of electoral votes and is augmented by a bonus system for votes cast in the preceding presidential election (Republican) or several elections (Democrat). The Republican party awards extra votes also if Republicans have won a state's governorship, United States Senate seat, or a majority of its seats in the House of Representatives.

Subject to general rules set by the national committees, each state is free to decide whether its delegates will be selected by party conventions or primaries. A few positions may be allotted to public and party officials. States using primaries to choose delegates doubled from fifteen in 1968 to twenty-eight in 1976, and thirty-five were scheduled for 1980. In 1976 about 78 percent of the Democratic and 70 percent of the Republican delegates were chosen in the primaries. In contrast, in 1968 about half of the delegates in both parties were named in caucuses. About 25 million people voted in the presidential primaries, but only a small fraction attended precinct caucuses.[2] Over 32 million people voted in the 1980 primaries.

Preconvention maneuvers   In recent times the nomination process has become a long-drawn-out affair. The New Hampshire primary in 1976

---

[1]There are many works dealing with aspects of the convention. One comprehensive work is by William R. Keech and Donald R. Matthews, *The Party's Choice*, The Brookings Institution, Washington, D.C., 1975. On rule changes in the 1970s, see Austin Ranney, *Curing the Mischiefs of Faction: Party Reform in America*, University of California Press, Berkeley and Los Angeles, 1975. For up-to-date changes, see *Congressional Quarterly Weekly Reports;* the August 4, 1979 issue, pp. 1609–1616, covers rules for 1980 delegate selection.

[2]Probably only a fraction of 1 percent to 5 percent. See Austin Ranney, *Participation in American Presidential Elections*, American Enterprise Institute for Public Policy Research, Washington, D.C., 1977.

took place during the last week in February, and the last primary was held in June. The first caucus was in Iowa in January. By June 1979 seven Republicans had formally announced their candidacy for the 1980 nominations, and some of them had raised over $1 million.

Where presidential hopefuls used to pick particular state primaries with care and avoided states where they might look bad, serious candidates now feel obligated to enter nearly all the primaries. The length of the primary season is such that one can recoup losses. This was true of Reagan in 1976. He did not do well in the early primaries but came on strong in the mid and later primaries. Actually he polled 50.5 percent of the total Republican primary vote but narrowly lost the nomination to incumbent President Ford.

As the nominations have more and more become media events, strategy dictates that a candidate try to win the earlier caucuses and primaries. McGovern in 1972 and Carter in 1976 were barely recognized in the polls before the Iowa caucuses and New Hampshire Primary, but successes there catapulted them into serious candidates if not front-runners. Although Carter edged Morris Udall by a mere 4,300 votes, he was declared the victor. Carter continued his strategy to establish his credentials quickly and force other opponents out of the race since they chose not to enter all the primaries. Out of a welter of early candidates Udall was the only one left by May. Although Governor Brown and Senator Church entered later primaries with some success, they were too late to overtake the front-runner Carter.

The role of the media is particularly vital in the earlier stages of delegate selection.[3] In what one observer calls the New Hampshire overkill, the television networks in 1976 carried an equivalent of 2.63 stories for each of the 38 delegates chosen, while in the important Massachusetts primary, which selected 147 delegates a week later, only 0.35 stories were carried.[4] Nearly always the person carrying the New Hampshire primary is viewed as front-runner, with pictures on the front page of weekly news magazines and much publicity. Winners seem to attract more space than losers. Pollsters pick a figure, usually a plurality, and a particular hopeful is adjudged the winner or loser with reference to the "expectation" figure of the poll. Winners also attract money and supporters, with an accumulative effect. Intended or not, the media are very important in the fortunes of candidates during the preconvention period. Carter captured only a plurality of 39 percent of the total primary vote but was the apparent nominee before the opening of the convention.

At the same time the winner of the most delegates in the primaries is not invariably the winner at the convention. Willkie (1940), Stevenson (1952), and Humphrey (1968) won without campaigning in any primaries. But primaries proved crucial to Eisenhower, Kennedy, McGovern, and Carter. Primaries are also important in eliminating weak candidates and, in a few cases, persons of stature, such as Muskie in 1972.

[3]For a comprehensive analysis, see James D. Barber (ed.), *Race for the Presidency: The Media and the Nominating Process*, American Assembly, Columbia University, Prentice-Hall, Inc., Englewood Cliffs, N.J., 1978.
[4]Ibid., p. 65.

With very few exceptions, candidates with 40 percent or more of the votes at the end of the first ballot have gone on to be nominated. Hence preconvention strategy dictates careful targeting to commit large numbers of delegates during the selective process in the state conventions and primaries because the trend is quite well established by the opening of the convention. Succinctly, candidates not only work with the "pros" in the party caucuses to capture delegates but are forced to reckon with the primaries and do everything possible to "look good" in the media and in the public opinion polls. Incumbent Presidents generally are assured nomination, but President Ford found that he had to battle in the primaries and use every opportunity to make news in order to fend off the serious challenge of Ronald Reagan. It is well to keep in mind, therefore, that every presidential election has a different strategic environment and that factors which obtained in 1972 or 1976 are not necessarily present in 1980 or 1984.

Rules change each four years, and the use of winner-take-all or proportionality at the congressional district and/or state level and the degrees to which delegates are bound may also have considerable influence on the fortunes of hopefuls.[5]

Composition of conventions   Earlier critics of the conventions saw them as composed of "a greedy crowd of officeholders," "unrepresentative," and often disreputable. Studies of delegates during the past generation have not found extensive corruption but that conventions, like legislative bodies, are not an accurate cross-section of their constituencies. Delegates tend to have more college education, come from a business or profession, and have above average income. Conventions also bring together large numbers of party and public officials.

Radical changes in the Democratic party rules in 1972 brought substantial departures in the demographic characteristics of the convention that year. In an effort to "overcome the effects of past discrimination," the rules encouraged state delegations to include minority groups, women, and youth in reasonable proportion to their presence in the state's population.[6] As shown in Table 7, the rule changes resulted in increased membership for certain groups. They also brought in many more inexperienced delegates (i.e., those not attending earlier conventions). To the distress of the old-timers, there were many fewer party regulars and activists and public officeholders than previously.

In 1976 the Democratic party backed off from the quotas with a consequent decline in youth, women, and black delegates. However, the national committee called for a 50 percent representation of women at the 1980 convention. Republicans in 1972 and 1976 were content only

---

[5]Winner-take-all means that the person capturing a plurality of the votes gets all of the delegates. Proportional representation means an approximation of voting and delegate allocation—for example, a person polling 15 percent of the vote will receive approximately 15 percent of the delegates.

[6]For aspects of these rule changes, see James D. Barber (ed.), *Choosing the President*, American Assembly, Columbia University, New York, 1974; Denis G. Sullivan et al., *The Politics of Representation: The Democratic Convention of 1972*, St. Martin's Press, New York, 1974, and Ranney, *Curing the Mischiefs of Faction*.

TABLE 7 Composition of national convention delegates, 1968, 1972, 1976 (in percent)

		Women	Youth (under 30)	Blacks	Hispanic	Indian
Democratic	1968	13	4	6	*	*
	1972	38	21	15	5	1
	1976	34	15	9	*	*
Republican	1968	17	1	2	*	*
	1972	30	9	4	1	1
	1976	*	*	*	*	*

*Not available.

Source: Data adapted from *The New York Times* and Ruth R. Scott and Ronald J. Hrebenar. *Parties in Crisis: Party Politics in America*, John Wiley & Sons, New York, 1979, p. 149.

to call upon the states for greater representation of various minorities. These resulted in more moderate changes. Under the rules for the 1980 Democratic convention, states are to elect an equal number of men and women; Republicans simply request states to do so. Also, Democrats require representation on the basis of presidential preference or uncommitted status. Republicans are not so required.

Organization and procedure   The first two days of the convention are occupied with such routine matters as adoption of rules, settlement of disputes over seating of rival delegations, and adoption of a platform. These activities are interspersed with the "keynote" address and flamboyant partisan speeches. Only rarely are there serious quarrels over credentials and platform planks. But the 1972 Democratic convention provided a spectacle of struggles over these matters. The credentials challenges set an all-time record, with most disagreement centering on whether the state delegation was adequately "representative" of minorities and women.

In adopting rules to assure openness, fairness, representativeness, and deliberation, the size of major committees at the Democratic convention was enlarged to 150. Meetings were open to the press and public. A smaller percentage of the resolutions committee could bring up floor amendments to the platform. This they freely did with the result of an all-night session debating platform.

When one considers the liberal rules, the convention showed remarkable decorum and delegates took their tasks seriously. Demonstrations were abandoned, and the hoopla characteristic of most conventions was missing. Yet the long debates were dysfunctional in several respects. Most notable was the long debate which delayed the McGovern acceptance address until the early morning hours, when most of the nation had gone to bed.

The 1972 Democratic revolution in the presidential-selection process and platform will be analyzed for many years to come and is bound to have impact on both parties. At the outset it showed in bold relief that rules are not neutral. They necessarily favor some contestants over others. The winner-take-all primary in California gave McGovern a bloc of 271 votes needed to bolster his cause. Selection rules diminished the representation of the regulars and officeholders in favor of candidate preference and to some extent the ideologically oriented. The rules established by the national party reduced the effect of state party rules and laws.

Because of the few militant reformers in the party, the Republicans had few battles over convention changes in the 1970s except for the formulas for state delegate allocation. Ford forces, fearful of a weakening of their support in the face of a powerful Reagan challenge, got through a "fair-play rule" requiring all bound delegates to follow their state's directions as indicated by the caucus or primary results. Reagan countered with a rule to require presidential candidates to announce their choices for vice-presidential nominee. Failure to do this would unbind delegates. The Ford people had enough strength to defeat the proposal on the convention floor.

The presidential nomination   After exhausting hours of bargaining over platform planks and many speeches, the convention turns to balloting. Some of the attributes of "available" persons, such as residence, religion, and experience, have undergone change in the past generation. With few exceptions, such as Willkie and Eisenhower, the nominee has served in elective public office. Residence in a large, pivotal state was considered essential for many decades, but this practice was abandoned in nominating Goldwater of Arizona, McGovern of South Dakota, and Humphrey of Minnesota. (Interestingly, however, all three lost the election.) Carter's nomination was a sharp geographical deviation as no person from the South had been nominated since before the Civil War. Moreover, Carter was, in terms of Washington, an "outsider." His nomination, which almost no one had foreseen six months before the convention, was due, as seen earlier, to his entry in almost all the primaries and to the support of Southern delegates. His preconvention primary successes resulted in removing Wallace, Jackson, and a long list of lesser contenders, such as Bayh, Shriver, Harris, and Shapp. Established figures but former losers such as McGovern, Humphrey, and Muskie did not contend in the primaries; Udall, who often ran second, failed to win a single primary; and Brown and Church entered too late to provide a serious floor fight. The mood of the nation in 1976 was anti-Washington, and Carter, as a new face, was able to capitalize on this in both his nomination campaign and his election campaign.

When balloting begins, the convention as a whole may be in the position of ratifying the obvious candidate and preceding with the "coronation" or in a position to make a decision. Keech and Matthews set up classifications to describe this phenomenon.[7] A "consensual" nomination is where a particular nominee faces no serious opposition, such as renomination of a President, exemplified by Roosevelt in 1936 and 1944, Eisenhower in 1956, Johnson in 1964, and Nixon in 1972. In some cases nonincumbents, such as Landon in 1936, Dewey in 1944, Nixon in 1960, and

[7]See ibid., chap. 6.

Reagan in 1980, were so far ahead that their nomination was essentially ratified. Reagan's successes in the early primaries led Senator Howard Baker to withdraw after only five primaries, Representative John Anderson after 15 primaries, and George Bush withdrew with 12 primaries remaining. After the final Democratic primaries Carter appeared to have enough to be nominated but Senator Kennedy continued his challenge at the convention. Then there were strong front-runners who were believed to be winners but who might be vulnerable should the convention get out of hand. Incumbents Roosevelt in 1940 and Truman in 1948, as well as Kennedy in 1960 and Nixon in 1968, fell within this "semiconsensual" framework. This also would seem to apply to Carter in 1976 and 1980.

Then there are a few instances where the convention appeared to be in a position of making a genuine decision because of factional conflict and complicating factors which did not make nomination of a particular person a sure thing. The nomination of Willkie on the sixth ballot in 1940 is the best example of this "nonconsensual" type during the last generation. But it applied also to Dewey (1948) and Stevenson (1952), both of whom were not chosen until the third ballot. The close contest in 1976 for incumbent Ford was extraordinary because, with few exceptions in history, Presidents have generally been accorded renomination without a serious struggle.

Vice-presidential nomination   The party nominee for President is customarily permitted to choose his running mate. Representative Charles Halleck of Indiana voiced reality when he said, "You don't run for Vice President. When a presidential nominee is named, he and the other party leaders sit around a room and select the vice-presidential nominee." Adlai Stevenson broke precedent by giving the convention freedom to select his running mate in 1956. Despite the popularity of the action at the time, both conventions in 1960 quietly reverted to former custom. The vice-presidential nomination is often used as a consolation prize to the losing political faction. It may be essential to assure collaboration in the campaign with disappointed, if not dissident, elements. In 1952 Nixon was instrumental in winning active support of Taft Republicans, and in 1960 Johnson played an essential role in carrying the South for Kennedy. Nixon's selection of Governor Spiro Agnew of Maryland in 1968 caused surprise and concern among many delegates. But Nixon felt that he had to carry some Southern states and that Agnew would be helpful in doing so. In retrospect the Nixon strategy paid off. The fiasco which replaced Senator Thomas Eagleton of Missouri with Sargent Shriver of Maryland after the convention hurt McGovern's cause.

In 1976 Reagan caused a stir when he announced his choice for Vice President in advance of the balloting for President and challenged Ford to do so. Reagan's naming Senator Richard Schweiker of Pennsylvania as his choice was denounced as a political ploy by the Ford people, and Ford refused to follow suit. Ford surprised the convention by choosing Senator Robert Dole of Kansas instead of Senate Minority Leader Howard Baker, who was believed to be a stronger candidate. Carter's choice of

Senator Mondale of Minnesota was generally popular with many delegates because it seemed to strengthen ties to the Midwest and the liberal wing of the party.

Many observers believe that selection of vice-presidential candidates should be given more serious consideration and that better methods should be used to appraise the candidate's competence. But the tradition of letting the presidential candidate name and impose his candidate at the convention is strongly entrenched.

Evaluation   Although national conventions became more sanitized when carried on television, they are still criticized for tedious speeches, much hoopla during demonstrations, their unrepresentative character, alleged backroom deals, and so on. But more important, perhaps, is that so many have expressed unhappiness with the nominations both for President and Vice President. Republican centrists were unhappy with Goldwater, just as Democratic centrists were displeased with McGovern. Antiwar youths disliked both Nixon and Humphrey. Right-wing ideologues believed Reagan would have been a stronger candidate than Ford, and many Democratic party regulars were dissatisfied with McGovern and Carter. At the same time, with few exceptions, those nominated were usually shown to be the preference of a large plurality, if not the majority, of the respective party's voters.

There has also been dissatisfaction with the vice-presidential selection process and some of the candidates chosen. The debacle of dropping Senator Eagleton from the McGovern ticket and substituting Shriver after the convention hurt the Democratic cause. The problems and eventual resignation of Vice President Agnew brought anew the problem of inadequate investigation of potential nominees. Senator Dole seemed to add little to the Ford cause, since he brought no geographical or other balance to the ticket.

What is often unappreciated is the fact that the preconvention process has sifted and winnowed out candidates, so that the delegates are generally removed from or greatly restricted in the selection of a presidential nominee and defer to his judgment in the vice-presidential choice. As noted earlier, the mass media campaigning, public opinion polls, and the extension of primaries have resulted in limiting the discretion of the conventions. The process itself does not assure that the nomination will go to one experienced in elective public office—witness Willkie and Eisenhower. Although in the past the conventions frequently turned to governors for their nominees, the choice of Carter led to criticism that he was a Washington outsider and lacked national and foreign experience. The logic of this would henceforth restrict nominations to members of Congress or cabinet secretaries.

A broader perspective recognizes that a convention is more than a nominating device. It usually results in a decision on the direction of the party leadership as between conservatives, liberals, and moderates. The conclave symbolizes the historic function of nomination by party activists. Even though conducted extralegally, the convention is a means of putting the stamp of legitimacy on the party's nominees for President and Vice

President and the national party platform. It is a useful instrument for catharsis, and generally, though not invariably, is followed by a momentary party cohesion during the general election.

The psychological aspects are not to be minimized. The affair is a great act of national party life. Party consciousness is whipped up as delegates are brought together from all the states and territories, and their ties to the national party are strengthened. Most go home and participate in the campaign with renewed enthusiasm; a few disgruntled, however, may sit out the election. A number of local leaders gain national prominence by their speeches or activities at the national convention. This may help them in their campaigns for public office.

Although platforms are widely regarded with skepticism, the national convention is a useful device for putting them together. It is an educational experience both for the delegates and the general public. Despite hyperbole some useful debates over platform planks have been carried to millions of viewers and added to the public's interest and education in national issues. Also, from the citizen's view, these colorful meetings are deeply embedded in American political life and psychology, and politics would be duller without them.

Thanks largely, but not entirely, to ferment within the Democratic party in the 1970s, the whole national convention process is in transition. Thousands of words have been written on party and convention reform. One set of changes relate to internal convention processes as the parties wrestle with better methods of resolving disputes over the seating of delegates—a historic problem. What should be the length of nominating speeches and demonstrations? What process and numbers of delegates should be required to offer floor amendments to the party's platform? The Democratic rules "opened up" opportunities for platform changes in 1972, with the result that the debates went on all night. So many people took advantage of the opportunity to make speeches that Senator Mc-Govern was unable to give his acceptance speech until after 2 A.M. Eastern time, and most of his audience was lost. The rules were dysfunctional in terms of overall party goals and exposure of the candidate. Parties are faced with the problem of imposing "gag" rules in the interest of reaching national audiences in prime time.

But perhaps the major problems are those arising from the delegate selection process. At one time reformers called for a national primary method of selection. With the great extension of primaries, along with some regional primaries, less support for the nationwide proposal has been heard. The problem then reverts to state legislatures and national party rules for decisions as to proportional representation, binding of delegates, and types of primaries, such as open or closed. Most students of government believe that the primary period should be shortened and that, to conserve candidates' energies and resources, regional primaries should be encouraged. But only legislatures can do this, and New Hampshire insists on being first and at least a week in advance of any New England primary. There will continue to be issues over "representativeness" of state delegations and disagreements over "true representation" of demographic groups. And to what extent will representation favor ideologues who often seem more interested in victory for an issue or a specific interest than in compromises which result in a victory for their candidate?

There seems to be little the parties can do, even if they wished, to diminish the role of the mass media during the preconvention period. The hopefuls will do everything they can to obtain favorable publicity amd exposure, and the primaries provide a greater opportunity than the caucuses to attain these ends. Yet, as we have said, rules are not neutral, and supporters of specific candidates will continue to manipulate them to promote their cause.

CAMPAIGN BEHAVIOR

American campaigns have a complexity and frequency not found elsewhere. The long ballot places candidates for state and local offices in competition not only with those of the opposite party but also with their own party's nominees in bidding for the voters' attention and campaign contributions.

There are many different ways of looking at campaigns. The electorate sees a campaign as an occasion for the airing and examination of issues. The voters then record their choices between rival sets of policies and solutions. Campaigns for public office are seldom plebiscites in this sense, as the two-party system rarely brings forth candidates with opposite positions on a wide range of issues. Rather, campaigns provide the voters with a chance to record their preferences as to which of two (or more) persons they want to hold public office. The function of the electoral outcome, then, is not so much to provide a mandate on issues as it is to choose rulers. But campaigns can serve the purpose of heightening interest in public affairs because they are usually conducted on the basis of a few strong issues.

Candidates and party leaders are likely to view campaigns as a form of political conflict with a general resemblance to an adversary proceeding. Contestants mobilize their resources and present their cases to the voters, but the competitors seldom have equal resources. Each candidate is engaged in trying to expand the coalition that gave him or her the nomination into a winning combination at the general election. A campaign in this sense is a process of coalition building. It aims to communicate a dominant image of the candidate that is more favorable than the image of the opposition.

Totaling up the whole complexity of a campaign situation is difficult but essential if a candidate and the candidate's manager are to prepare the master design of strategy. To plan an effective campaign involves (1) developing strategy, (2) controlling issues, (3) building organization, (4) exploiting nonmonetary assets, (5) selecting techniques, (6) judicious use of media, and (7) raising money. These are interrelated and interdependent.

Factors in campaign strategy   When devising strategy, the candidate's personal resources are carefully appraised. These include one's public record if any, background, reputation, relationships with the press, civic leaders, and one's own party's hierarchy, and access to interest-group support, financial contributions, and advertising firms. A candidate's relationship with other persons on the ticket and the competence of personal entourage are also of importance. The primary and general election campaigns are usually integral operations. If an aspirant has maneuvered the primary campaign so as not to alienate opponents, their support may be most helpful in the general election.

Situational factors over which a candidate has little control profoundly influence techniques and strategies. Those of special significance are whether one is an incumbent or a challenger, and the strength and weakness of one's opponent. The socioeconomic characteristics of the district, degree of two-party competitiveness, and voting habits (straight or split ticket) of the constituency will influence the types of appeal. To some extent the types of campaign appeal are determined by the character and expectations of the electorate. If a candidate believes that appeals to class, race, or local prejudices will be effective, there is a temptation to use them, especially in close contests. Since election days are fixed, some issues may be manufactured if natural ones have not arisen at campaign time.

Every campaign is different. Certain variables, however, tend to remain the same. For example, we saw earlier that turnout is greater in presidential years than in midterm elections. Voting is greater for President than for Congress, for governor than for state legislature. Incumbents have enormous advantages—though incumbents at times do lose. New issues and factors arise. Some 25 million potential new voters, ages eighteen to twenty-four, entered the electorate in 1972, and the reduction of residence requirements to thirty days facilitated exercising the franchise for many migrants. The Vietnam war was a very important part of the strategic environment in 1968 and 1972. Although Ford had the advantage of incumbancy he was faced with disadvantages, including the unpopularity of the pardon of Nixon. Because of high inflation and unemployment rates, the state of the economy rather than foreign policy became dominant in the 1976 campaign. Continued high inflation, the decline of the dollar, and energy problems assured that management of the economy would be a basic theme in the 1980 campaign.

Campaign strategies   Because of the electoral college winner-take-all system, a presidential candidate winning the twelve largest states is close to the magic 270 electoral votes needed to be elected. Much of the candidate's effort and personal appearances are directed toward winning these and medium-sized states, while reaching the others by media.[8]

[8]Literature on campaign strategies and techniques is extraordinarily abundant. Books are available on specific campaigns; perhaps best known is the series by Theodore H. White under the title *The Making of the President*, which was continued from 1960 through 1972 and published by Atheneum, New York. A few general works are Nelson B. Polsby and Aaron B. Wildavsky, *Presidential Elections*, Charles Scribner's Sons, New York, 1976; Robert Agranoff, *The Management of Election Campaigns*, Holbrook Press, Boston, 1976; Dan Nimmo and Robert L. Savage, *Candidates and Their Images: Concepts, Methods, and Findings*, Goodyear Publishing Company, Pacific Palisades, California, 1976, and by Nimmo, *The Political Persuaders: The Techniques of Modern Election Campaigns*, Prentice-Hall, Inc., Englewood Cliffs, N.J., 1970.

Nixon's so-called Southern strategy, with appeals for conservative change, paid off handsomely in 1968 and 1972. In the former campaign he avoided a head-on clash with George Wallace for fear of alienating the South. Nixon also gave little help to Southern congressional candidates so as not to hurt his cause with dedicated Democrats who consistently supported their party's candidates for Congress. In June 1972 the President did minimal campaigning, leaving the burden to "surrogates" prominent in his administration. The surrogates placed McGovern on the defensive and were helped by a well-funded Democrats for Nixon Committee headed by former Texas Governor John Connally. The general strategy was one of portraying McGovern as favoring changes that were too radical, bumbling the Eagleton affair, and waffling on issues. In the face of having to defend an unpopular regime and problems with the economy, Ford chose to stress his experience. He ran against Congress as well as Carter, and pointed with pride to his many vetoes of "bad" measures passed by a Congress Democratically controlled. (Interestingly a large number of incumbents and candidates for Congress also ran against Congress.)

Carter began his general election campaign substantially ahead of Ford in the polls. His problem was to try to win Southern votes which had gone to Nixon and Wallace and strengthen the traditional Democratic vote elsewhere. His strategy was to emphasize the need for a new face and new programs which would benefit ethnic and other minorities, provide tax and governmental reforms, and so on. He talked in general terms and strongly emphasized issues of integrity and restoration of faith in government and public officials. Like many other candidates he struck antigovernment and antiestablishment themes. In the final analysis Carter's victory was comparatively close. He lost several large Northern states, such as California, Illinois, New Jersey, and Michigan, and all of the West except Hawaii, but this was offset by his carrying every Southern state except Virginia and by his marginal victories in New York, Ohio, and Pennsylvania. The third-party campaign of former Senator Eugene McCarthy appeared to have cost Carter Oregon, if not one or two other states.

A candidate's use of and relationship to the rest of the ticket is likely to be determined by pragmatic and expedient considerations. There is a team emphasis where candidates see profit in it, otherwise strategy and campaigning are individualistic matters and follow the dictum "vote for the man." Campaign managers of local candidates appraise the strength of presidential and gubernatorial nominees before deciding whether to conduct a "coattails" campaign. In parts of the South, Democratic candidates for Congress have frequently felt it better to disassociate themselves from the presidential nominees. Many Republican candidates completely separated themselves from Goldwater's cause in 1964.

Campaign managers are making increased use of public opinion polls to ascertain the voters' perceptions of the parties, candidates, and the issues; the results of polls often profoundly affect strategy. From a manager's point of view, the electorate consists of hard-core voters and workers, the party sympathizers (weak Democrats and weak Republicans), and the independents. Each does not necessarily respond to the same appeal, and so the approach must be flexible. "Breaks" and nonrational factors often crop up during a campaign and may be very important.

Presidential campaigns, like others, seek to activate the indifferent and uninterested, reinforce the partisan, and convert the doubtful. The three major elements to be worked into the campaign strategy are party, candidate, and issues. The degree and place of emphasis on each calls for a high order of understanding, intuition, and perhaps luck. As the majority of the electorate has a party preference, strategy is necessary to persuade the partisans to come to the polls. Stevenson, Kennedy, Humphrey, McGovern, and Carter were much less well known than their Republican opponents. All emphasized the Democratic party label and appealed to Democrats to stay with the party by voting for them. Early in this campaign, Kennedy said, "No Democratic candidate for the President has ever run and said 'Parties don't matter' because we are proud of our record."

Most campaigns are won or lost by marginal changes in the political alignment. Parties are the broadest reference group and changes in political faith are slow. The minority party is likely to conclude, therefore, that it is easier to sell candidates and issues than to change voter attitudes toward their party. Eisenhower, Nixon, and Ford were faced with trying to hold their partisans and then to siphon off enough weak Democrats to be elected in both campaigns. Nixon played down his party connections; he played up the candidate and personality angle. Candidates try to stay on the offensive. An incumbent, nevertheless, can hardly escape defense of his record. In so doing, he may more or less ignore his opponent and operate from the strategy of a superior position, as Franklin D. Roosevelt did in his three campaigns for reelection and as Eisenhower did in 1956 and Nixon in 1972. The traditional pattern in nearly all campaigns is to emphasize repeatedly one's strong points and ignore those of the opposition. This tactic helps to reinforce and activate partisan preferences and predispositions.

Timing is a particularly important aspect of strategy. Eisenhower's last-minute promise that he would "go to Korea" injected new vigor into the 1952 campaign and implied he had an approach that might mean early termination of the war. As the underdog, Humphrey picked up much strength in the waning days of the campaign by denouncing Nixon's "silence" on issues and featuring the strength of his running mate, Senator Edmund Muskie, in contrast to Governor Spiro Agnew, who ran far behind Muskie in public opinion polls. Henry Kissinger's announcement a few days before the election that "peace was at hand" probably helped solidify the Nixon contention that the war was about over. In recent years, a saturation media-oriented campaign has characterized the closing days of the contest. Spot announcements and other features presumably reach the confused, the wavering, and those whose minds are not yet made up.

Campaign organization Campaign machinery is intimately bound up with the strategy of selling the party, the candidate, and the issues. The regular organization is activated, vacancies are filled, and a volunteer corps recruited to assist in the headquarters. Its job is to accentuate the party aspect by getting the party's propaganda before the voter and beseeching party regulars to "vote Republican" or "support the Democratic ticket." Its particular emphasis is arousing and reinforcing the strong partisans and standpatters. The regular party organization is usually strongly preoccupied with the state and local ticket, and it often falls to auxiliary groups to give special assistance to the presidential nominee. Young Democratic and Republican clubs are useful to concentrate on new voters. Though rarely appreciated by outsiders, many activists, both in campaigns and in other aspects of party life, are motivated by the desire to maintain their own power in the party. Charges have been made that some elitists are prepared to subvert their party's ability to win an office if winning would undermine their own hold over the party and over the benefits of party power.[9]

Recent developments have undermined the campaign role of the regular party organization. Nonpartisan elections, the entry of public relations, advertising, professional pollsters and statisticians, mass media, and the tendency of candidates to mobilize their own organizations mean that the party mechanisms no longer monopolize the electoral process. The exigencies of the separation-of-powers system make for a multiplicity of elected offices and the proliferation of campaign machinery and finance committees. Limitations on contributions by individuals and on expenditures for federal candidates by single committees have resulted in decentralization of campaign organization. Labor political-action committees, for example, usually conduct campaign activities with their own funds, and a business group may pay for a television broadcast. A number of voters have an antiparty or nonparty bias that will not respond to the symbols of the party.

It is particularly important to reach the opinion leaders in the community and the active minorities in interest groups, those who have influence over the opinions of fellow organization members and friends. These persons and their followers are often reached through two types of so-called independent citizens associations. Organizations of this type are also designed to win the votes of independents, waverers, switchers, and weak partisans on both sides. Campaign committees with nonpartisan titles (often the creation of the party organization) may be able to reach them with a reference-group appeal, an issue, or a personality emphasis. Cross-pressured voters may be stimulated by nonparty committees to support a particular candidate without feeling they have deserted their party.

A second type of nonparty group may be composed of persons of a particular social or economic class and is directed more pointedly to issues concerning them. Committees of doctors, farmers, lawyers, educators, veterans, blacks, and many similar groups appeal to their members, often with emphasis on issues, to ignore party lines and to vote for a candidate because that person is deemed best for them. Permanently constituted organizations, such as the AFL-CIO Committee for Political Education and Americans for Democratic Action, likewise enter the campaign, usually with emphasis on the presumed policy differences between candidates.

[9]For a rather extreme statement of bipartisan collusion in some elections, see Walter Karp, *Indispensable Enemies: The Politics of Misrule in America*, Penguin Books, Baltimore, 1974.

Finally, candidates have a personal entourage which in many cases displaces the party and nonparty groups in terms of determining master strategy and the general direction of the campaign. Nixon's White House group worked personally with the Committee to Reelect the President. It bypassed the Republican National Committee and operated quite secretly in raising funds and determining campaign strategy, including the well-known "dirty tricks" and techniques that were later aired in the Watergate hearings.

The proliferation of campaign organizations results in confusion, duplication of effort, and, often, bad feeling between the party regulars, the amateurs, the volunteers, and professional campaign managers. Yet decentralization comprehends a theory of voting behavior which permits a great many persons to participate in a campaign in a way that reflects each individual's interests. Multiple organization permits particularization on specific issues or the candidate and may be an important source of finance.

The new campaign technology of outside professionals brings skills in polling, voter profiling, and media use. Computers are now widely used for major offices to keep records of resources, donors, and manpower, to prepare personal communications by means that make them appear to be individually typed and processed letters, and to maintain and retrieve enormous amounts of data. The new campaign politics has further eroded the role of parties in campaigns and has made electioneering increasingly expensive.

Techniques   Much transformation has taken place in presidential campaign methods. The torchlight parade was attributed to Andrew Jackson, and the "whistle stop" campaign became a major device with the spread of railroads after the Civil War. From miles around the depot, people poured in to see and hear the nominees. In the 1920s, radio made it possible for the voices of the nominees to be carried a greater distance into homes, and the masses of voters could be reached by a single speech. The 1950s brought a further revolution with the advent of television and the jet plane. Adlai Stevenson set a new style and new record by traveling 2700 miles in one day! Television added the opportunity to "project the image" through sight as well as sound. Candidates' families, monster parades and rallies, as well as the nominees themselves, are now brought to the home screen. Fast planes permit the nominees to hold a breakfast meeting in Cleveland, have lunch in Chicago, stop mid-afternoon in Denver, and preside over a soiree in San Francisco. A furious pace of stepped-up, automated campaigning in which each headquarters builds up a corps of transportation, publicity, communications, and subject-matter specialists characterizes modern presidential campaigns.

Large sums of money are invested in television appearances, which also have undergone much change since 1952. There is a tendency toward fewer half-hour speeches by the candidate and toward more use of the one- to five-minute "spot announcement." This has the advantage of leaving regular programs untouched and keeping a "captive" audience which might otherwise turn off the set.

The use of media to reach voters is a problem of balance, and no one mode is relied upon. The electronic devices have not entirely replaced rallies and campaign literature, bumper stickers, buttons, and so on, in presidential campaigns. But in 1976 Carter and Ford found that expenditure limitations required them to reduce literature in favor of using more money for television.

For offices such as state legislatures and local councils, radio and television tend to be uneconomic. Here the old-fashioned techniques of doorbelling, coffee klatches in private houses, and pieces mailed to those registered are widely used. For almost every level of office, telephone calls to voters, reminding them of registration deadlines and, on Election Day, to check for voting, are conducted by hosts of volunteers.

The techniques used, of course, are restricted by the resources available and by the strategic position of the candidate and environment. An incumbent's publicity stresses the favorable aspects of his or her record and may ingore the challenger.[10] Challengers usually find that they must attack the record of the incumbent and stress the qualities they possess that would enable them to do a better job. Those in office try to avoid being placed on the defensive, and both the ins and the outs sometimes operate on the premise that the best defense is offense. The Nixon campaign was especially successful in placing McGovern on the defensive, so that the 1972 election, to a considerable extent, turned out to be a referendum on McGovern rather than Nixon.

The publicity in many campaigns—perhaps more at the local than at the presidential level—is often characterized to some degree by name calling, guilt by association, innuendo, and misrepresentation and, at times, by varieties of "dirty tricks." "Big spender," "reactionary," "left-winger," and "tool of the bosses" are a few of the well-worn phrases often creeping into campaign publicity. Quotes of opponents may be taken out of context, and statistics are especially susceptible to manipulation. For example, the challenger assails the "ins" by saying that more persons are unemployed than before and the incumbent proudly says that more people are employed than ever before. Actually both statements may be correct.

Most candidates avidly seek endorsements from respected figures—environmentalists, scientists, educators, physicians, attorneys, and the like. Generally, but not invariably, endorsements by labor unions and business associations are sought, but at times a candidate does not feature them lest he or she be charged with being a tool of a special interest.

Face-to-face television debates, especially for statewide and national offices, are on the increase. Some candidates would like to avoid them but fear to do so. Presidential debates were abandoned after the Kennedy-Nixon contest in 1960 because the incumbent Presidents preferred not to participate. In 1976 the Kennedy-Carter debates appear to

---

[10]For a comprehensive and informative account of the styles and strategies used by congressional incumbents seeking reelection, see *Congressional Quarterly Weekly Report*, July 7, 1979.

have enhanced the positions of both candidates, for they were less well known and they were given a chance to demonstrate their knowledge of national affairs.[11]

Money in elections   The price tag on political campaigns has increased rapidly since 1860, when Republicans reportedly spent $100,000 to elect Lincoln.[12] In 1972, in a massive fund drive, more than $60 million was raised by the Nixon-Agnew ticket and about half that amount for McGovern-Shriver. McGovern became the most expensive loser in history! Senator Jesse Helms of North Carolina spent $6 million on his reelection in 1978. Successful Senate candidates averaged $617,000 in general election expenditures in 1976. Senator George McGovern spent nearly $10 per vote in seeking reelection in 1976 and won by a modest 53 percent of the vote. In 1978 House and Senate candidates spent $153 million, a cost far exceeding inflation.

Although these figures appear staggering they compare favorably with some other nations. Japan and Sweden greatly exceed the money spent in the United States on a per capita basis. Further there are substantial variations in campaign costs. Some candidates for House seats have won in a competitive election with less than $25,000, while the two major-party candidates in one California district in 1976 collectively spent over $1 million. These figures may be compared with a nationwide average of $80,000 for a House seat in the same year. State legislative races, even within the same state, usually show sharp variations. S. I. Hayakawa won a hotly contested California Senate Republican primary race in 1976 with less than $100,000, while his two opponents each spent over a half-million dollars.

In a pluralist society, group interests hope to gain access to government by assisting their friends to get elected. Campaign donations are a form of political participation. The myriad of regular party and separate candidate committees has greatly decentralized campaign financing. It becomes difficult, therefore, to get an accurate picture of receipts and disbursements. The recent adoption of public disclosure and reporting laws in the states and for Congress will henceforth make it possible to ascertain the amounts and sources of campaign moneys. Aggregate estimates are that $200 million was spent nationally in 1964 and that the figure rose to $425 million in 1972. With public financing of presidential election costs and limitation of general-election expenses to $22 million per candidate, much less was spent by presidential candidates in 1976.

[11]See George F. Bishop, Robert G. Meadow, and Marilyn Jackson-Beeck (eds.), *The Presidential Debates: Perspectives and Promise*, Praeger Publishers, New York, 1978.
[12]The literature on campaign finances is very extensive. Among the many works by Herbert E. Alexander, see especially his *Money in Politics*, Public Affairs Press, Washington, D.C., 1972, and *Financing Politics*, Congressional Quarterly, Inc., Washington, D.C., 1976; for materials on the states, see his *Campaign Money: Reform and Reality in the States*, The Free Press, New York, 1976. See also David W. Adamany and George E. Agree, *Political Money*, Johns Hopkins Press, Baltimore, 1975. The *Congressional Quarterly Weekly Reports* carry extensive accounts on campaign finance for national offices. For 1978 spending, see the report for September 29, 1979, pp. 2151-2163.

Why costs rise   The spectacular increase in campaign expenditures is caused by many factors. One is the growing size of the electorate. But expenses have increased in much greater proportion. Inflation is one of the culprits, with long-time staples in the campaign pantry, such as travel, printing costs, postage, and campaign buttons, skyrocketing. The changing technology brought about by the onset of television, computers, data processing, polling, and much greater use of professional campaign firms has sent costs soaring. Many formerly safe districts have become more competitive, especially in the South, where Republicans have mounted serious campaigns for governor and for Congress. The shift to candidate-structured politics has also increased the amount and importance of money in the electoral process.

Some characteristics and effects   With conspicuous exceptions, incumbents tend to outspend challengers in state and local elections, primarily because they have greater fund-raising resources. However, a Federal Election Commission study of the 1976 elections found the margin of congressional incumbents' spending quite small.[13] But winning costs more than losing—winners spent 62.4 percent of the total. The Commission also found that Democrats outspent Republicans $32 million to $28 million, but there were more Democratic candidates. Studies of state races and of presidential campaigns before partial public financing in 1976 generally show that Republicans tend to outspend Democrats. Candidates supported by business and labor have tended to have an edge over others. Recently this has diminished as educational, medical, and single-issue groups are giving more contributions for specially targeted districts. As will be seen shortly, new campaign finance laws in the 1970s are changing the anatomy of contributions. Little change is taking place in the advantages for wealthy candidates who heavily subsidize their own campaigns and need to spend less time and money raising funds. John Heinz of Pennsylvania spent $600,000 of his own money in 1976 and narrowly won the primary contest against two financially strapped opponents.

Struggles for solutions   The attentive public and legislature have grappled with the old saw that "Money is the mother's milk of politics." So far as campaigns are concerned there have been two general options. One is stricter controls and regulations and public reporting of sources of contributions and expenditures. The other is the fostering of greater equalization of resources by helping candidates to meet their legitimate campaign needs, such as public financing, minimal free media time, and space in a voters' pamphlet mailed to all registered voters. The second option is especially helpful to independent and third-party candidates, who have great difficulty in obtaining campaign money for public exposure.

The legislatures and Congress have struggled with diverse types of regulations only to see interested parties find loopholes in the new laws. Tougher public disclosure laws, adopted in the early 1970s, showed

[13]Summarized in *Seattle Post Intelligencer*, October 2, 1977.

enormous contributions from special-interest "fat cats." These laws plus the revelations of Watergate led to several important changes in the election laws in 1974 and 1976.

Highlights of these provisions include limiting a person to a maximum donation of $1,000 per candidate in a primary, runoff, or general election, a possible total of $3,000 to any federal-level candidate, and an aggregate total contribution of $25,000 in any one election year. A person may make unlimited "independent expenditures," such as placing an advertisement in a newspaper, but the expenditure must be shown as an action independent of the candidate. A person may also give up to $20,000 to a national party provided the money is not earmarked for a particular candidate.

Each organization or political-action committee is limited to $5,000 maximum per candidate, but there is no aggregate limitation. An organization may give as long as the $5,000 per candidate limit is observed. The Democratic and Republican senatorial committees are permitted to give $17,500 a year to a candidate. The 1974 law also placed spending limitations on congressional candidates and personal spending by candidates, but these were declared unconstitutional in a historic decision by the Supreme Court in January 1976 (*Buckley v. Valeo*). The provisions limiting candidate expenditures, therefore, were struck down, with the result that wealthy candidates can spend their own money as they wish and the aggregate amounts spent on congressional races can continue to mount.

Although the law has resulted in keeping individuals or groups from giving huge amounts of money to one candidate as in the past, it has not reduced special-interest contributions. The law permitted companies to solicit campaign contributions from employees to be expended through political-action committees (PACs). Since 1974 there has been a phenomenal rise in the number of PACs created, and the amounts raised and expended. The number of PACs rose from 608 in 1974 to 1360 in 1978; contributions rose respectively from $12.5 to $32 million. About half of the PACs were founded by corporations. However the largest single donor was the American Medical Political Action Committee, donating $1,645,000.[14] Labor unions have long used the PAC device, and corporate and labor groups each funneled about $10 million to congressional candidates in 1978.

One fairly important result of the law is the making available of enormous amounts of data, so that the media and the public now have a much better picture of who is giving to whom. (In effect all contributions and expenditures of $50 or more must be reported periodically to the Federal Election Commission.) The data is also useful to candidates since they can learn where their opponents are obtaining money and how it is being spent.

Because candidates must place less reliance on a few large gifts, a number of them are turning to fund-raising agencies that resort largely to requests by mail. Large sums of money are now being raised in this

[14]On PAC giving, see *Congressional Quarterly Weekly Report*, June 2, 1979, pp. 1043–1045. See also the issue of April 8, 1978 and *The New York Times*, April 19, 1978.

way from single-issue and ideological groups. These donations, small in amount but large in number, are of consequence to many candidates.

As of 1978 some eight states were conducting experiments with limited public finance in the form of a checkoff provision on state income tax forms, with the money going to parties or to individual candidates. Overall the amounts raised have been disappointing, but they have helped to defray the costs of party headquarters and other expenditures. Full public funding has not been adopted in any state because of both ideological and practical considerations.

Public financing of presidential elections began in 1976 with money collected through the checkoff plan, which is optional for those filing income tax returns. After their nominations, both Carter and Ford received close to $22 million for the general election campaign and could use no private sources. The respective national committees were allowed to spend a limited amount of money in their candidate's behalf.

To assist candidates in the presidential primaries, the federal government provided matching funds after a contender raised $5,000 in each of twenty states, with $250 being the maximum individual contribution that was matched by federal money. By law, no candidate could receive more than $5 million or spend more than $10 million in the preconvention period. Reagan received the maximum, Ford $4.7 million, Carter $3 million, and Brown $374,000. Altogether, major-party candidates collected more than $23 million in matching funds. Although minor-party candidates were eligible for public funds in the general election if they received 5 percent of the total vote, none of them qualified. Not surprisingly the law has been criticized by third-party candidates. The public financing law made for austere spending compared to previous elections, but the press called it one of the cleanest elections in history, and the Ford and Carter organizations could not be accused of using "marked" or "special-interest" money.

The states and Congress have long struggled with the problem of campaign resources. The American ethos says that money should not be the sole determinant of who wins public office. Challengers and competition are to be encouraged, and candidates are finding that their parties are no longer in a position to provide the major portion of campaign funds. Private interests want to give directly to the candidates rather than to national committees. For nonpresidential offices, money to conduct primary campaigns is especially crucial to challengers who may not be well known; state laws have been of little help to them. From a democratic perspective, enough money is needed to alert the electorate, to project information about the candidate, and to critique the performance of incumbents. Laws have often been referred to as "incumbency protection," but it is difficult to enhance the causes of challengers by law.

THE USES OF CAMPAIGNS

Classical democratic theory views a high degree of participation and involvement in a campaign by all classes of citizens as highly desirable. As has frequently been noted, the evidence does not indicate that this goal has been realized. On rare occasions large percentages of people vote, but comparatively few of them donate to campaigns or become active in parties or political interest groups. Some political campaigns have inflamed passions by demagogic tactics and have stirred deep rancor between parties, classes, and candidates. Character assassination, "smear" politics, appeals to bigotry, falsehood, and the threat or use of force negate the democratic process and make consensus difficult after the election is over. Public expectation or acceptance can exert much influence on the level of campaign oratory and publicity.

Many voters deplore the lack of clear-cut contests on issues, policies, and programs, saying that campaigns result in confusion rather than clarification. But the basic purpose of an election is not a plebiscite on policy matters but a decision on who shall rule. It seems doubtful that campaigns should be regarded as suitable occasions for decisions on specific issues. At the same time, it is appropriate for a campaign to contain some rational discussion of the problems facing the community.[15] This includes the presentation of information and analysis of the public's problems and the possible results of alternative solutions. It would expose the approaches and views of the parties and candidates and help to clarify areas of both agreement and disagreement between the contestants. Effective political deliberation implies that neither side has a monopoly of the communications media.

Political discussion that maximizes the achievement of consensus is regarded as "rational." A good campaign is one that leaves officials and interest groups free to conduct between-elections negotiations to arrive at consensus over program. The free society faces continuous problems in the waging of contests over who shall control government. One of the most important but by no means the only question is how to provide adequate resources for bringing candidate, party, and issues before the public. Closely related is the problem of developing ethics and rules of the game that will be respected by voters, parties, and candidates alike. Despite the occasional use of questionable tactics and irrational appeals, most campaigns arouse civic interest, bring aspirants before the voters, give many persons an opportunity to engage in the excitement of electioneering, and provide some clue to differences between candidates and parties. In the American pluralist society, pressure groups, political parties, citizens' associations, opinion leaders, public officials—indeed nearly all of us—have a stake in the political game and can influence either its improvement or its malfunctioning. The effectiveness of the complex political system in the future will depend, as in the past, on the successful interaction of all these components.

REVIEW QUESTIONS

1 Which type of system would you prefer for nominating a candidate for Congress—convention, closed, open, or blanket primary? What

[15]For a discussion of this point, see Stanley Kelly, Jr., *Political Campaigning: Problems in Creating an Informed Electorate*, The Brookings Institution, Washington, D.C., 1960; and Gerald M. Pomper, *Elections in America: Control and Influence in Democratic Politics*, Dodd, Mead & Company, Inc., New York, 1968.

impact would the preferred method have on the relationship between the candidate and your local party organization?

2 Do party officials in your county actively participate in primaries? If so, how? Is this a good idea?

3 What rules or guidelines would you recommend for the allocation and selection of delegates to national conventions?

4 Would the type of person chosen and his or her qualities of "availability" differ if a nationwide presidential primary were used instead of a national convention?

5 One writer asserts, "We have moved into a new political era in which the old rules and axioms no longer apply." Evaluate this remark in terms of relevancy to (a) campaign organization, and (b) campaign methods and techniques.

6 State at least four principles or values that should govern the raising and spending of money in campaigns. What methods of campaign finance and what regulations would help to realize these values?

7 What are the purposes of campaigns? Can you establish priorities for the fulfillment of these purposes? What criteria would you use to judge whether a given campaign served a high or "rational" purpose?

8 On several occasions the authors have raised questions about the applicability of the classical theorist's concept of the political individual. Prepare a refutation or answer to the view or a thesis in defense of it.

6 PRESSURE-GROUP POLITICS

At the beginning of Chapter 4 we noted that politics and the shaping of public policy are decentralized, infinitely complex matters. They have their irrational aspects as well. Although quite aware of their interests, many citizens are rather ignorant of how they may be satisfied. Personal desires may be confused with political programs. To this point we have taken note that political parties, however vaguely, appear to link citizens to the government. Elections also connect votes to popular control of public officials. Parties and elections are symbols of democracy. It is now time to look at the third tie between citizens and public policy—interest groups. The Constitution itself sets the stage for a flourishing pluralist society in providing for freedom of speech, press, and assembly, and the right of citizens to petition their government. In a free-market economy, many private decisions, such as pricing, sales, production, and distribution policies of large national and international corporations (as in the case of the oil producers' cartel), have great impact on public policy. At times it is difficult to distinguish between "public" and "private" decisions.

GROUP POLITICS AND SOCIETY

Omnipresence of interests   In 1787, James Madison in *The Federalist* stated that "a landed interest, a manufacturing interest, a mercantile interest, a moneyed interest, with many lesser interests, grow up of necessity in civilized nations, and divide themselves into different classes, actuated by different sentiments and views." A half century later, that keen observer of American life, Alexis de Tocqueville, saw Americans as an amazing people who "constantly form associations." He saw not only the organization of economic interests but also "association of a thousand other kinds, religious, moral, serious, futile, general or restricted, enormous or diminutive."

Madison saw the latent "causes of faction" inherent in man, which manifest themselves in the unequal distribution of property, in zeal for differing opinions, and in affection for different leaders. Interest groups exist in all societies, but their organization, operation, and emphasis differ from country to country. One of the characteristics of Western democracies is that they are pluralist societies in which interest groups are free to form and press for certain government policies, often cooperating with or opposing other organizations with different values, goals, and aspirations. The regulation and arbitration of these competing forces of society are, indeed, a major task of government.

What is "group" politics?   Let us realize at the outset that "group interests" and "organized groups" are not synonymous. It is a mistake to think of interest and organization as one same thing. Most families, friends, neighbors, and coworkers have common interests but are rarely organized with recognized leaders, yet these groups have great social significance in terms of serving social, economic, psychological, and other needs. These primary groups are excluded from our discussion here since they were considered in Chapter 2. Our focus is mainly on political interests that are expressed through organizations.

"Interest group" and "pressure group" are often used interchangeably. All pressure groups are interest groups, but not all of the latter are pressure groups. When an organized group decides to bring its case to government, it becomes a pressure group or political interest group.[1].

A very large number of groups have little or no political program, and only a handful of organizations are formed exclusively to influence government. Some occupational groups form subsidiary or separate political-action committees to promote specific political goals. This leaves the parent organizaton free to promote the social, economic, and other nongovernmental objectives without being labeled as a political organization, which, in some cases, would be a liability. Churches, medical societies, business, labor, and agriculture are among those which often have separate political-action groups.

So far as political interests are concerned, the American pluralist society is not equitably organized. Moreover, there are unequal degrees of interest in the collective good on the part of rank-and-file members. There is more of a tendency to organize along producer lines than consumer lines, although consumers are better organized today than formerly. Nearly everyone is worried about inflation. But anti-inflation interests are not well organized. Furthermore, the pressures for self-aggrandizement by some groups have contributed to increasing costs, and anti-inflation forces have not enjoyed continued success in combating them. Similarly, citizens are interested in the prevention of crime, but there are few private organizations whose reason for being is fighting crime. Society generally discountenances vigilantes because of their excesses. There are many other causes where one cannot find either an organization or leaders with political clout to promote them. Peace is an almost universal interest, but there are no huge, well-funded organizations working for it. Until recently, those seeking job equality, clean air,

[1]Harmon Zeigler defines a pressure group as "an organized aggregate which seeks to influence the content of governmental decisions without attempting to place its members in formal governmental capacities." See *Interest Groups in American Society*, Prentice-Hall, Inc., Englewood Cliffs, N.J., 1964, p. 30. A highly recommended general work is James Q. Wilson, *Political Organizations*, Basic Books, Inc., New York, 1973.

and certain improvements in the quality of life were unable to find effective organizations for these purposes.

At the same time a number of causes are supported by people who receive no direct selfish gain. Few persons belonging to the League of Women Voters and promoting good government do so because they seek personal economic profit. In societies to abolish capital punishment, one would not find persons convicted of murder. The point is that not all private organizations seek benefits only for their own members. There are many charitable and "public interest" associations which try to advance the general welfare or welfare of a particular disadvantaged group. Others are engaged in trying to advance an ideal, a philosophy, or a philanthropic interest other than tangible economic profit. Many people, however, prefer not to join any organization, although some find themselves forced to become members in order to protect their economic interests. Others voluntarily become members of an organized association for highly diverse reasons.

The traditional "group theory" has come under attack in recent years.[2] The argument that organized groups exist to further the common interests of all their members and to serve their personal and individual interests is being reexamined. Too often overlooked are the small groups that differ qualitatively as well as quantitatively from large groups.[3] The smaller the group, the more likelihood that it will bring a greater share of the total group benefits to the individual and subsets of individuals. Often purely personal or individual interests can be advanced by individual action outside of an organized group. As Olson points out, there is "no purpose in having an organization when individual unorganized action can serve the interests of the individual as well or better than an organization."[4] In a word, one does not have to join an organization to realize certain desires and goals.

THE SOCIOLOGY OF THE
PRESSURE SYSTEM

Composition of membership The inclusiveness of membership in formal associations is extraordinarily varied.[5] The overwhelming majority of musicians belong to the American Federation of Musicians. Until recently the overwhelming majority of physicians belonged to the American Medical Association, but a much smaller percentage of lawyers are members of the American Bar Association. It is estimated that only 6

---

[2]A thoughtful work is that of Macnur Olson, Jr., *The Logic of Collective Action: Public Goals and the Theory of Groups*, Schocken Books, New York, 1968.

[3]See ibid., chaps. 1 and 2. Olson believes that relatively small groups are more effective than larger ones.

[4]Ibid., p. 7.

[5]E. E. Schattschneider points out, in *The Semi-Sovereign People*, The Dryden Press, Hinsdale, Ill., 1975, that the range of membershp in organized identifiable groups tends to be quite narrow.

percent of American automobile drivers belong to automobile associations. Public opinion polls show that no more than one-third of the farmers belong to any farm organization. A small percentage of blacks belong to associations designed specifically to represent them. Most veterans do not belong to veterans groups, and an infinitesimal number of consumers belong to consumers' leagues.

Careful analysis of the membership claims of group leaders is likely to show a considerable number of members who have little more than a "paper" connection. They pay little or no attention to the group's activity and may even be out of sympathy with it. Chances are that they are often in arrears on their dues and inactive in the organization's affairs. Large numbers of other studies tend to support findings that many organized groups touch only a few people in a community. The American practice of "joining" is not as universal as popularly assumed. Group participation is related to social and economic status (SES). People on the lower SES levels are less likely to belong to any organizations than the people on high SES levels. Thus, participation in voluntary groups tends to have an upper-class bias, with a very large number of people remaining outside the stream of pressure politics. Even a considerable number of upper-class citizens are inactive and are for one reason or another not represented by a group. Politics often becomes the affair of smaller cliques. While an interest as a whole may not be well organized, specific subinterests are. This is especially true of business, with its trade associations, the diverse commodity associations in agriculture, and trade unions.

The active minority   Even a superficial look at an organized group reveals that its decisions and affairs are in the hands of a small number of activists. The larger the group the smaller is the percentage of those in charge. Even at small-group meetings, attendance is commonly disappointingly low in terms of the "democratic" model of large participation. Literature on the leadership of groups of diverse sizes is abundant; space permits only a few generalizations. Formal organization itself usually creates the leadership positions and agencies. Sometimes the bylaws succeed in placing authority in the hands of a certain group, such as a board of directors, executive committee, or house of delegates. An annual convention may be the sovereign authority but obviously cannot function as the day-to-day leader. Thus real leadership may be exercised by persons other than those formally designated. The internal structure of large organizations is complex and often best understood by the paid officials, executive secretary, or permanent bureaucracy. Their knowledge and skills give them an advantage in terms of making decisions, which are later "ratified" by the members. Moreover, the financial structure of the group may be such that the key positions are held by the persons with the greatest control over finance. The opposite can also be true where leadership falls to those having the leisure and personal security to labor for the organization with little or no remuneration.

Some persons have leadership qualities that inspire confidence. If these persons obtain power, operate successfully, and dramatize the conflicts with other groups, they often remain in control a long time. Leadership is a relationship between the leader and the led. Even though leaders may become somewhat separated from their constituents, their role vis-à-vis other groups may secure their position. If they are perceived by their own followers to be successful pressure politicians with the government and fighters of the good fight against competitors, the position of leadership may be long assured. The active minority may need at times to exaggerate the dangers from outside in order to secure its position and preserve internal cohesion.

Every political interest group has three areas of contest: intragroup, intergroup, and government. Some interest-group politicians are concerned with all these; in other cases specialization permits some of the active minority to devote their primary effort to one rather than all areas. One of the great problems of the pluralist society is that of internal governance. To what extent is, or can, the leadership be democratically controlled? Do the leaders speak with authority for the membership? Are the group's programs, as formulated, truly in the best interests of the group? Can and should the rank and file play a larger part in making decisions? Are adequate mechanisms available to bring about changes in leadershp and program?

In an earlier chapter, the "reference" function of groups was mentioned. Groups may provide members with values, explanations, and rationalizations for their political behavior, viewpoints, and voting. Persons may find that conformity is the price of acceptance by their groups. Group leaders and the activists have the function of articulating group goals and seeing to it that the organization performs these functions to the satisfaction of the bulk of the membership.

The elite become the opinion leaders. Preservation of their position and of the group itself dictates that they combat the erosion potential in the cross-pressures of those members who belong to other groups. Factionalism endangers cohesion. In performing their roles, the active minority is differentiated from the others in the group by a higher rate of participation. But this is a matter of degree, for the activist group undergoes change as other members constantly move in and out of the leadership positions. And leaders remain leaders only if they have a reasonably successful relationship with the rank and file.

Although the active minority brings the maturity and experience necessary for effective representaton, it may, at times, be dysfunctional. By control over official publications, the agendas of the meetings, and the formulation of referenda and other matters submitted to the membership, the leaders may limit or remove consideration of alternative points of view. This may serve the interests of the leaders but not necessarily those of the membership or those aspiring to rise to leadership positions within the organization. Another liability may arise when the leaders espouse policies or take the organization into causes not supported by the membership. Public officials and outsiders may claim that the leaders do not reflect the views of the group, resulting in weakening its overall position.

Discussion among political scientists has swirled around the interpretation of power as related to public decision making. We cannot enter into the extensive dialogue save to point out that groups are woven into all of the theories.[6] Simply stated, the pluralists see political decisions as the outcome of a plurality of many competing interests. Elitists, on the other hand, argue that major decisions are made by a comparatively few unrepresentative persons in an undemocratic manner. Both tend to see society as clustered in functional groups some of which are more influential than others. The democratic elitists are the in-group rulers who are in a position to make decisions, subject to certain traditions, broad limits, and elections which may replace one group of elitists with another. Pluralists maintain that it is impossible for any one group to become dominant. But the emergence of large-scale hierarchical organizations and many of lesser scale has, however, altered the classical pluralist ideal of voluntary association.

MAJOR ORGANIZED INTERESTS

Interest groups may be classified by origin, such as economic, ethnic, religious, or political interest. Or one might try to classify them by general purpose or by the means they employ to attain their goals—lobbying, public relations, electoral activities, and so on. There has been a tendency to organize around occupational categories, and these groups are likely to be the largest and most visible. But, as will be seen, there are a great many other competing groups which generate issues. Let us not forget as well that governments are also interest groups. After looking at some of the major categories of organized interests, attention is turned to the diverse methods of operation and application of political pressure short of becoming a political party.

Business   The modern corporation stands head and shoulders over any other association of American private enterprise. Labor and agriculture have also developed into big enterprises for organizing aspects of economic life. Commercial and financial interests were first to organize, and today there are more national organizations of business than of any other group.[7] Businesses and industries of every size and description have organized. Trade associations had local antecedents in early America, and their scope was extended to the national and regional levels beginning with the Civil War. They proliferated especially rapidly from 2,000 in 1920 to 12,200 in 1950, though the great majority were subnational in scope. Associations of a single business, such as the National Association of Broadcasters, the National Retail Dry Goods Associa-

---

[6]For a comprehensive treatment and evaluation of these theories, see G. David Garson, *Power and Politics in the United States: A Political Economy Approach*, D. C. Heath & Company, Lexington, Mass., 1977.

[7]National and local organizations run into the thousands. A list of the former is found in the *Encyclopedia of Associations: National Organizations of the U.S.*, Gale Research Company, Detroit, Mich., 1964. Supplements are issued to keep the list up to date.

tion, the United States Brewers Association, the American Bankers Association, and the Edison Electric Institute, are designed to promote and protect the interests of those engaged in the respective trade throughout the nation. One of the most powerful and well-financed groups is the American Petroleum Institute. It is an association of 350 oil and gas companies and thousands of individual members. It has a huge budget and has been in the center of many battles over energy, such as pipeline construction and excess profits tax on the oil industry. Much of the work of associations of this type is not related to government, but when public proposals affecting them surface, their leaders go into action.

The National Association of Manufacturers was formed in 1895. It is composed of individual firms and is much concerned with governmental actions, such as tariffs, trade promotion, and labor relations. A second great national federation, the Chamber of Commerce of the United States, founded in 1912, is built upon 2,500 trade associations and state and local chambers of commerce. It has referred to itself as the spokesman for business and conducts a referendum among its members to ascertain their viewpoints on a large number of issues.

Even though the attitudes of business are highly respected in government circles, it is easy to overstate the cohesion of business interests. A lack of unity exists between the small individual entrepreneurs, small businesses, medium-sized businesses, and the great industrial and manufacturing giants, between the independent retailers and the chain stores, and between businesses heavily concerned with lending money and those with borrowing it. Each may go to the government seeking help or protection against the other. Yet it is around public policy that organized business is often able to weld what unity it enjoys. All business-people can be induced to support programs against tax increases, especially on business, and government interference; and also programs for the curbing of big labor, the protection of business from foreign competition, and the enhancement of business. Today the list of legislative objectives, both for and against public action, is becoming increasingly lengthy.

Labor   Labor had local organizations long before it made attempts at national federation after the Civil War. The Knights of Labor gave way in 1886 to the American Federation of Labor, which was largely based upon craft unions but admitted the unskilled. The Congress of Industrial Organizations, founded in 1935, emphasized "vertical" or "industrial" organization of members who work in the same industry but not necessarily at the same craft. The AFL and CIO merged in 1935. Either because of being expelled or by choice, a number of powerful groups, such as the Teamsters, the Railroad Brotherhoods, and the auto and steel workers, remain independent of the AFL-CIO. Organized labor thus suffers internal dissensions and permits outsiders and politicians at times to play off one group against the other. Nevertheless labor unions are a significant force in American politics and have about one-fourth of the labor force in their membership. Public-employee organizations are enhancing their membership and power, and energetic efforts are being made to organize migratory farm workers.

During the 1930s labor moved from a faith in unfettered collective bargaining as a means of attaining better hours and working conditions to seeking positive legislation. It supported and saw enacted a long list of social and regulatory measures. It continues to seek extension of social insurance programs, including health. Labor was often frustrated by what it called the "farmer-lawyer-merchant-dominated" state legislatures and became more active at the national level. There are a great many more business than labor associations, so that the former have more contacts with government. Also, labor has concentrated on major issues while business has exerted pressure on a broad range of topics. As will be seen later, the tactics of the two interests are quite different.

Agriculture   In the present century many representatives of agriculture have advocated government intervention for crop reduction, marketing arrangements, price supports, and public loans, varying from short to long term, to buy seed and to purchase heavy equipment. Farmers have sought rural electrification, protection from certain competitive foreign imports, and "parity" with industry in the prices they receive. Agricultural interests look to government for assistance because they are more subject to nature's hazard than any other group. As the number of small family farms declines, large industrial farms grow, and a disparity exists between the commercial farmer and the family farmer. There is also a sharp disparity of income within the agricultural community itself and between agriculture and other occupations. Black farm families pose a special problem in rural poverty, even though tenant farming is on the decrease. Marginal farmers seek government programs that will help them stay in business even though the nation has huge crop surpluses.

These characteristics of the agricultural economy produce deep cleavages and many spokesmen purporting to champion agriculture. The term "farmer" may refer to the small dirt farmer, the farm owner living in the city, livestock breeders, dairy interests, rice producers, or growers of corn and fruits. Many of these occupational interests are represented in commodity associations, such as the National Beet Growers Association and the California Walnut Growers Association, which function much like trade associations. There are three major federations attempting to speak for the farmers. The National Grange, formed shortly after the Civil War, is fraternal in approach, dedicated to enhancing the social and intellectual life of the farmer. Today it speaks for many dairyworkers and for a moderate to right-of-center approach on many public policies.

In 1902 low-income farmers started the Farmers' Union, and its center of gravity has remained with the marginal farmers and the "left." It has worked with labor unions and supported social legislation. Newest and largest of the agricultural groups is the American Farm Bureau Federation, which was started with the assistance of the U.S. Department of Agriculture in 1919. The Federation was to assist in coordinating and helping the county farm bureaus. At present the Federation speaks for the more prosperous farmers and occupies a generally conservative position compared to the Grange and Farmers' Union. Today the family farm is nearly over. The number of farms has decreased radically as the average acreage per farm has increased. The size of the so-called farm vote has dwindled, and the legislative reapportionments since 1962 have reduced farm representation in the state legislatures. But commercial farming has become big business along with the growth of huge cooperatives. Farm associations still pack much influence in Congress, and enormous outlays for agricultural programs are continued in the federal budget.

Professionals Profressionals have long had associations to impose standards, keep out the untrained, and "elevate the profession." At their inception most professional societies were dedicated to "avoiding" politics. As happened in the labor movement in the 1930s, the leaders of the various professions have recently undergone a change in perception and now stress the economic relevance of politics. The legal profession has been well represented in legislatures and did not need to employ extensive lobbying or participate in elections. But with no-fault insurance and many other proposals, many local lawyer associations have become more active in politics.

Perhaps the greatest change has taken place in the field of education. Public education, by its very nature, requires positive action from government, including unpopular tax and appropriations measures. Popularly elected officials who must act upon school funding and policies are keenly sensitive to political considerations. Parent-teacher associations along with school administrators have increased their efforts to publicize the case for adequate school support and are referred to as the "school" or "education" lobby. Until the 1960s the battleground was largely limited to the local and state levels. In 1972 the National Education Association (NEA) abandoned its policy of avoiding political involvements. It became aggressive not only in trying to increase federal aid to education (adopted in 1965) but to give teachers more decision-making authority and higher salaries. The NEA and its state affiliates spent $3.7 million on election campaigns in 1974. NEA and its allies, including the American Federation of Teachers, have pressed for the teacher's right to strike. Teacher strikes became rather common in the late 1970s, and there was one strike of college professors at Boston University. While labor unions have generally been openly Democratic, the education groups have tried to retain a nonpartisan posture.

A controversy over the "politics of health" has raged since the 1930s and seems certain to continue throughout the 1980s. Medical care has become a big business and a larger share of the consumer's income is going for medical services. Medicare went into effect in 1966 and greatly increased the government's role in organizing and financing the distribution of health services. Labor, consumer groups, and many officeholders have supported a public health-insurance plan. Opponents have profited by the inability of Congress to agree upon one of the many diverse plans and meet the heavy costs of the program. One of the most effective opponents is the American Medical Association, which has bitterly attacked most plans. As noted elsewhere the AMA, through political-action committees and lobbying efforts, has been influential in thwarting efforts for a national program. It has allies in auxiliary groups, such as hospital interests, nurses, and pharmacists.

OTHER INTERESTS

We have just noted some examples of major economic interests pursuing political objectives by going beyond the immediate needs of servicing the membership. These groups usually receive a lion's share of the publicity, but hundreds of other groups have at least some political goals. Veterans' organizations, for example, moved into areas such as pensions, bonuses, and vocational rehabilitation which called for public action. Currently the American Legion, formed after World War I, has attracted a large membership; it has supported the GI Bill of Rights and has taken positions on foreign policy and internal security. The American Veterans Committee, formed after World War II, has lobbied for social legislation, in contrast to the more conservative Legon and the Veterans of Foreign Wars. Senior-citizens' groups are being increasingly politicized as they try to get more assistance for their financial and personal security in the face of mounting inflation. Tocqueville's observation that for every new undertaking in the United States "you will find an association" is not invariably true, as there are many unorganized interests. Yet one must be impressed with the increased political activity of the older organized groups and the creation of new ones. Mention should be made of some other categories of organized interests that have come into political prominence.

Ethnic and religious groups   Ethnic, racial, and religious minorities are especially concerned with public programs related to their desire for social betterment, equality of opportunity, and freedom from discrimination. Blacks particularly have sought governmental assistance in order to gain their social, economic, and political rights. The National Association for the Advancement of Colored People (NAACP) is best known as a politically oriented group seeking to abolish restrictions and discrimination which interfere with the rights of black Americans. Only a small fraction of blacks belong to the NAACP, and there is disagreement among blacks on the degree and types of militant political action. A number of newer groups boast increasing memberships as they become associated with rising protests. Most notable of these are the Southern Christian Leadership Conference, People United to Save Humanity (PUSH), and Soul City. The Black Muslims, as an ultramilitant group, have reacted against the conservatism of black leadership but have not built up a large following. The National Urban League seeks to improve employment opportunities for blacks by working directly with employers.
    The influence of blacks offers an important example of the fact that an

organization's power is not always to be equated with its size. At the same time blacks are one of the few major ethnic groups to have no significant influence on foreign policy, and they make little attempt to influence the government toward Africa. However when black UN Ambassador Andrew Young resigned under fire in 1979, black leaders said they would try to interest their fellow ethnics to pay more attention to the Palestinian problem in the Mideast and to African affairs. In contrast American Jews pay little attention to domestic issues relating particularly to Jews, but they are a powerful force on United States policy in the Mideast. The American Israel Public Affairs Committee is an umbrella organization that represents every segment of the American Jewish community and can mobilize a network of activists whenever Israel-related issues arise.

Civil rights has become a burning issue at all levels of government. Many new groups which represent American Indians, Spanish Americans, and Asian Americans have formed. Several have been successful in drawing attention to their plight and their underrepresentation in government and in private groups. Militant students groups at times have become involved off-campus with the causes of ethnic minorities. Women's-rights organizations are becoming increasingly active in support of equal opportunity legislation and objectives and in the struggle for or against the adoption of the Equal Rights Amendment.

Notwithstanding the American doctrine of separation of church and state, many churches are vitally concerned with public policy, and many of them have formed social and political auxiliaries for the purpose of educating their memberships and, often, to take positions on policy issues. Humanitarianism is one reason for the churches' concern with civil rights, social justice, and welfare legislation. Certain public policies, such as Selective Service, fluoridation, aid to parochial schools, ownership of property for investment, birth control, abortion, gambling, and liquor, may directly impinge upon church tenets; in such instances the churches may speak out through the pulpit or through an organization, such as the National Catholic Welfare Conference or the National Council of Churches of Christ, and hundreds of local church groups. As in all groups, some members take sharp exception to their church's activities in the political realm.

Public-interest and single-issue groups   A theme running through pressure-group literature is that the stronger lobbies in Washington have economic objectives. But there are also noneconomic organizations formed to speak for a general public interest. The Sierra Club and diverse recreational agencies are mobilized to protect and expand wilderness areas. Environmental and ecological councils are teaming up with other groups to fight those who would relax pollution controls and regulations. Common Cause, founded in 1970, affords an example of an organization whose purpose is to lobby for governmental reform. Its focus has been on Congress and some state legislatures to bring reforms in campaign financing, "open" government, lobby registration, and legislative procedures. It has given some attention to tax and other policies. It is allied with liberal organizations and has had considerable success in bringing about changes in governmental structures and procedures. Perhaps the best-known consumer and general-interest activities are those of Ralph Nader and his organization, Public Citizen Inc. These consumer.and self-styled public-interest organizations cut across political, social, and occupational lines.

Elsewhere reference has been made to the use and effectiveness of single-issue groups with political objectives. These groups are not new, as witness the abolitionists and prohibitionists of the past. But they are important today because of their number, membership cohesion, zeal, and high salience, and many are well financed. The anti–gun control and anti-abortion forces and those wishing to repeal the rights of homosexuals enjoyed a number of conspicuous successes in the late 1970s.

STRUGGLE FOR INFLUENCE: OUTSIDE GOVERNMENT

Public relations   The techniques that groups use to exert influence depend on their size, internal cohesion, leadership, and financial resources. Whereas labor may be able to mobilize a sizable vote from among its own members, businesspeople cannot because of smaller numbers. Business, however, has superior financial resources. It has the ability to employ the best legal talent, and its cases before public agencies are carefully prepared, urbanely presented, and possessed of a *savoir-faire* often lacking in the presentations by other groups. Business was the first important group to utilize public relations with marked success, and this remains a major, if not the most important, technique of business.

Briefly, public relations activities of an organization are carried on (1) to curry favor with the general public, so that it will react sympathetically toward the organization and favor its general goals, (2) to rationalize the group's goals in terms of the public interest, (3) to neutralize criticisms of the opposition, (4) to attract support from other groups that might share its objectives, and (5) to mobilize the rank-and-file membership behind the leadership.

Radio, television, and the periodical press afford interest groups an opportunity to reach persons outside their own membership for purposes of creating favorable images and attitudes toward them. Business has been highly successful in eliciting general approbation from white-collar and professional workers. Notwithstanding their critical comments about certain businesspeople, millions of Americans outside industry subscribe to the view that what is good for business is good for the country—a tribute in part to the public relations program of business. The medical societies have evoked favorable images of the "men in white" and the self-sacrificing family doctor. The essence of this type of public relations is the rationalization of one's own goals in terms of the public interest. By "lobbying" the public through publicity, private groups may bypass powerful party leaders and public officials. In this process, certain groups are advantaged and others disadvantaged. Less affluent groups, such as migratory workers, are less able to afford expensive television time and slick-paper magazines than business and most professions. Public relations resources are unequal, and those who cannot afford them must find compensating devices or be handicapped in mobilizing segments of the public in behalf of their goals.

Often overlooked in consideration of the "propaganda" or "education" outputs is the fact that they are frequently directed to the membership as well to the public. Their purpose is to promote loyalty to the cause, bolster sagging morale, reinforce the myths of the group, and explain complex issues to the membership in understandable terms. Such "education" may help to convince the rank and file that "headquarters" is doing its job and fighting "the good fight."

Confrontations and demonstrations   Although not a new technique in American politics, overt demonstrations have been in special vogue since the 1960s. Civil rights organizations made much use of sit-ins, freedom rides, pickets, and voter registration rallies during the 1960s. Peace marches were common until 1973; they still appear sporadically. These marches are aimed at the general public as well as at public authorities. Many, if not most, demonstrations result in publication in the media and often are set up for that purpose. In front of television cameras cattlemen killed calves and buried them to dramatize that they were receiving insufficient prices.

Degrees of force and violence accompanied some of these tactics, leading to confrontations between police and the protesters. In more extreme cases there has been looting, arson, serious bodily assault, heavy property damage, and even loss of life. Street battles have occurred over busing of schoolchildren. A few political groups have grabbed hostages and demanded money or other restitution for their release. The hostage system in international politics has witnessed the murder of ambassadors and innocent bystanders. These incidents have led to a review of violence as a political technique and efforts by public authorities to cope with it—often without success. Society must try to meet legitimate grievances, so that the aggrieved do not feel compelled to resort to violence to attain ends. This "crisis in authority" is one of the great challenges of modern times.

Party relationships   Political parties and pressure groups are organizers and controllers of power. This is why the parties and certain groups show a high degree of interdependence. Parties need group support in order to elect their candidates and maintain them in power. Organized groups with political objectives find parties useful to gain access to those in public authority. The parties and the political groups share power and influence, and their interests, objectives, and methods sometimes resemble each other so much as to make them indistinguishable. But the membership of parties, such as it is, is larger than that of any one organized group, and parties propose candidates for office, whereas the great functional groups rarely do. Parties must appeal to a broad spectrum of interests and avoid identification with one group to the exclusion of others.

Pressure groups and parties may have contact through financing, influencing of platforms, personnel, and electoral activities. Most financial support for parties and candidates is raised through private donations. Even in the face of legal restrictions, the members of pressure groups (if not the groups themselves) are heavy donors to candidates and to parties.

In the previous chapter we noted the great increase in political-action committees and the large sums they raise and expend in campaigns. Most of their money does not go to party committees but directly to candidates. A number of groups cover their bets by giving to both Republicans and Democrats. Special interests trying to preserve and enlarge the favored treatment they receive under tax laws contribute heavily to many members of the House Ways and Means Committee. In order of size, contributions in 1974 came from the oil and gas industry, real estate, securities, banking, public utilities, and the trucking industry. In contrast, labor gave much less but helped those serving on labor and welfare committees. Railroad interests contribute to members of the Commerce Committee, which has control over regulatory legislation. Next to the American Medical Association the milk industry gave the most money to the 1976 campaign because of its interest in limiting dairy imports and maintaining federal price supports for milk. The Watergate investigations and public disclosure laws make the public increasingly aware of potential and actual conflicts of interest and of the influence of money in politics.

In the 1800s and first part of the twentieth century, workers and farmers experimented with their own political parties but enjoyed few successes. Blacks did similarly in parts of the South in the 1960s, and Spanish Americans have polled some votes for their candidates under the La Raza Unida label in Texas. In 1978 the antiabortionists polled enough votes under their own Right to Life party in New York to earn a future place on the ballot as a full-fledged minor party. In the main most groups have not found the third-party route a rewarding one in terms of electoral successes and are more likely to put their effort and money into supporting major-party candidates sympathetic to their cause.

Pressure groups try to influence party platforms. Spokesmen for interest groups submit briefs and oral arguments before the resolutions committees of the national conventions. The formulation of state and county platforms affords perhaps even more opportunity for groups to be influential and to receive publicity for their views. The platform is a method by which a political party can build a coalition of supporting interest groups, and pressure groups in turn can remind officeholders of platform pledges.

The relationship between a nonparty and a party organization varies from place to place, but the general looseness of party organization makes it relatively easy for members of interest groups to become active members of parties. Political interest group leaders usually make a point of becoming personally acquainted with party leaders, candidates, and officeholders. Sometimes members of an organization try to win nomination for one of their own in a party primary. Both the political right and left have at times successfully infiltrated local party organizations by capturing precinct positions and delegates to conventions. In some areas labor unions have moved into the Democratic party organization in such numbers as to be able to dominate the state platform, convention, and organization. Indeed in some communities organized labor is identified with the Democratic party, and business and medical groups are similarly viewed as adjuncts of the Republican party. Pressure groups have at times taken control of minor parties, such as the Prohibition, Populist, and Farmer-Labor parties, but they usually find that third parties seldom give them the desired access to government. Today pressure groups largely concentrate on influencing the programs espoused by the major parties and their candidates, leaders, and officeholders.

Perhaps the most important relationship between pressure groups and parties develops during campaigns. Legal requirements force labor's Committee on Political Education to construct a parallel organization, but it is far more common for an interest group to cooperate closely with party leaders and candidates than to set up duplicate campaign machinery. Pressure groups are often not interested in the entire ticket and prefer to concentrate on certain offices and create a pressure group–candidate relationship rather than a pressure group–party relationship. The groups provide workers to get voters registered and to serve at the polls on Election Day. Organizations may "lend" some of their staff to party and candidate headquarters during campaigns and encourage their own members to participate actively by canvassing, distributing literature, ringing doorbells, talking with neighbors, and attending rallies.

For diverse reasons, party organizations often avoid direct assistance to a candidate in a contested primary. Under these circumstances a candidate seeking nomination may find pressure groups willing to give assistance if he or she is friendly to them and has some chance of winning. A primary campaign can serve as a forum for criticizing an incumbent and as an educational medium on some issues. Several groups make public endorsements, both in primaries and in general elections. Labor union and other journals commonly print roll-call records of incumbents, rating them "right" or "wrong" from their organization's viewpoint. Endorsement may give candidates exposure in their constituencies and make them acceptable to other groups. Some candidates, fearing endorsement would have an opposite effect, prefer no publicized support.

Two other types of election afford opportunities for pressure-group influence. One is the nonpartisan primary and election in which candidates run for local offices without a party label. Functional groups can and often do back candidates without the liability of being labeled pro-Republican or pro-Democratic.[8] Members of the bar often endorse can-

---

[8]For example, Gerald Pomper found evidence in the Newark, N.J., nonpartisan municipal elections that ethnic pressures may be substituted for those of party. "Ethnic and Group Voting in Nonpartisan Municipal Elections," *Public Opinion Quarterly*, vol. 30, pp. 79–97, Spring 1966.

didates for judgeships, just as educational associations endorse candidates for school superintendent. Nonpartisan candidates are usually not recipients of direct aid from party organizations and are likely to be in particular need of nonparty support. In both partisan and nonpartisan campaigns, only a minority of pressure groups openly participate. Many more work cautiously and indirectly behind the scenes. Leaders and groups of persons within an organization may be active and encourage others to be so but are quick to proclaim that they either "do not speak for the organization" or are participating in the campaign unofficially "on their own." Many organizations judge it expedient to be friendly and to cooperate with both sides by officially embracing neither in a campaign.

Pressure groups often wholeheartedly and officially take part in campaigns on constitutional amendments, city charter changes, and initiative and referendum measures. Such campaigns are seldom left to the unorganized. These affairs are costly, and much of the money is put up by organized interests. Initiatives on "right-to-work" proposals pitted the powerful labor and management contenders against each other; millions of dollars have been spent in several states to "educate" voters for or against such proposals. Huge sums have been spent by industry— sometimes with help from labor unions—to defeat initiatives placing restrictions on the building and expansion of nuclear facilities and requiring bottle deposits. Limitations on property or other taxation by initiative spread to a great many states after California adopted Proposition 13 in 1978. Liquor, gambling, and morals issues also provide the subject matter for ballot propositions. Dummy or front organizations, using labels such as "Save Our Children Committee" and "People's Committee for Clean Waters," may represent a specific group interest which feels it more discreet to campaign other than through its regular organization.

STRUGGLE FOR INFLUENCE: IN GOVERNMENT

Lobbying the legislature   Former veteran congressman Emanuel Celler of New York once defined lobbying as "the sum of all communicated influences—both direct and indirect—on legislators concerning legislation," and said it was "indispensable to effective lawmaking" and "the bloodstream of the democratic process." Since legislation is the result of compromise and the accommodation of interest-group demands, the conscientious lawmaker wants to hear from all interested parties and recognizes the legitimacy of pressure politics.

Because of the complexity of the legislative process, the techniques of access vary over a period of time and from bill to bill. Bicameral legislatures offer innumerable stages from bill introduction to final passage to defeat or emasculate a proposal. Conversely, the sponsors of new legislation must win a series of victories, and lobbying becomes a continual process. The cards are stacked more in favor of opponents than advocates. Most citizens are unaware of the great amount of defensive lobbying by those whose theme in legislative corridors is "leave us alone" or "don't do it." Representatives of organizations frequently find mobilizing the membership around a "threat" or "moral" question advantageous.

When organization leaders ascertain whether their posture is to be defensive-negative or offensive-positive, they commonly mobilize the membership on behalf of an "official" position. This provides the rank and file with legislative goals and enables the leaders or hired representatives to speak with "authority" for the organization. From this the group agents utilize various means to take their case to the legislature, including (1) preparing statements for and providing information to legislators, (2) personal contacts with legislators and their friends, (3) grassroots communications, (4) alliances with other groups also pursuing legislative objectives, and (5) formal contacts at critical points of the legislative process such as committee hearings, the rules committee stages, voting, and conference committee.[9]

Spokesmen for groups have facts, figures, and interpretations on how proposals can or do affect their constituents. The larger groups generally have permanent research staffs to mobilize data and at times even to draft bills for legislators to introduce. One of the most important weapons of the lobbyist is the possession of information which the lawmaker needs. This is especially true in state legislatures, which lack the same expertise found in congressional staffs. But even members of Congress are in need of data possessed by representatives of private groups. One of the problems is to provide equal access to all sides, so that the legislator has the necessary information and viewpoints to make a reasonable decision.

Successful lobbying usually begins long before the opening session of the legislature. Officials of the pressure organization or hired lobbyists try to get acquainted with the candidates during the campaign and often assist them in their efforts to get elected. These personal friendships are "renewed" both before and during the session by means of cocktail parties, dinner, golf games, and so on. Personal friendships are prime factors in the legislative and all decision-making processes. Friendships provide lobbyists with access to, if not influence with, lawmakers and are assiduously cultivated. Some of the most effective lobbying is done with legislators who are already identified with the pressure group; hence the representatives of the organizations are working with their friends and allies in the legislature. Many legislators are members of veterans', riflemen's, law, labor, farm, and business associations and work from within the legislative halls for their groups' goals. They provide information to

[9]Three general works on the interactions of interest groups with the various branches of the government are Carol S. Greenwald, *Group Power: Lobbying and Public Policy*, Praeger Publishers, New York, 1977; L. Harmon Zeigler and G. Wayne Peck, *Interest Groups in American Society* 2d ed., Prentice-Hall, Inc., Englewood Cliffs, N.J., 1972; and Norman J. Ornstein and Shirley Elder, *Interest Groups, Lobbying and Policymaking*, Congressional Quarterly, Inc., Washington, D.C., 1978.

their member lobbyists, who relay it to the group leaders. (Group spokesmen will admit, at least privately, that one of their big jobs is lobbying their own people.)

As a result of information directly from the legislators, and on initiative from the group's leaders, a "press the button" drive may be ordered to exhort the membership to write, wire, and or phone. The National Rifle Association, with some 850,000 members, claims it has produced more than a half-million letters, postcards, and telegrams within seventy-two hours.[10] Several senators reported receiving more letters on gun control in 1969 than on any other single bill. Grass-roots influence can be exerted through persons back in the district upon whom the legislator depends for information and for financial or other support.

Rarely does a pressure group have the field to itself. It is in competition with other groups for votes and influence. Therefore, success usually involves working alliances between associations to obtain support or at least neutrality. Sheep ranchers may support a tariff on tin if the tin interests will support a tariff on wool. Some groups, such as the National Rifle Association, have such broad memberships that they can defeat regulatory measures. One United States senator was quoted as saying: "Most of us are scared to death of them. They range from bus drivers to bank presidents, from minutemen to four-star generals, and from morons to geniuses, but they have one thing in common: they don't want anyone to tell them anything about what to do with their guns, and they mean it."[11] Nowhere is the process of working together better demonstrated than in river and harbor improvements and defense expenditures, where legislators from different areas support each other's projects.

Finally, lobbyists are present at every stage of bill passing to present a formal position. This includes committee hearings, before roll calls, calendar preparation, and the conference committee. The most competent legislative agents are those who know the loci of power and influence within the legislature and have rapport with the key legislative leaders, because many wavering members take their voting cues from the leadership. Experienced agents working for groups appreciate the importance of timing and the dynamics of the legislative process itself as well as the self-interest and motivations of the lawmakers.

The efforts of a particular organization are probably not as successful as popularly believed. Bauer, Pool, and Dexter, in their study of foreign-trade groups, raise doubts about the effectiveness of a single pressure organization. In their study of tariff legislation they found the lobbies poorly financed, "ill managed, out of contact with Congress, and at best only marginally effective in supporting tendencies and measures which already had behind them considerable congressional impetus from

[10]For an informative account of the lobbying and public relations activities of this group, see Richard Harris, "If You Have Your Guns," *The New Yorker*, April 20, 1968; and Robert Sherrill, *The Saturday Night Special*, Charterhouse Books, David McKay Co., New York, 1973.

[11]Harris, reprint pp. 4–5.

other sources."[12] At the same time, don't sell short the influence of combinations of great economic interests. The lobbies of these groups are by-products of the organizations having the capacity to mobilize the membership for diverse purposes. Because they function for the members in nonlobbying capacities, it perhaps helps the lobbyists to speak with greater authority on lobbying objectives.

Working with administrators   Much legislation originates with interest groups and in the office of administrative agencies at all levels of government. Private groups and administrators often work together on a program to be submitted to the legislature. Executive-agency lobbyists try to weld intergroup coalitions behind department bills. Interest groups are concerned with good working relationships because in the administration of policy, many lower-level but important decisions are made. Contacts by interest-group leaders with the legislature are usually sporadic, whereas those with administrators, in many cases, are continuing and constant.

Many bureaucrats gain power through being identified with clienteles and interest groups. At one time the Veterans Administration was referred to as "the institutionalized expression of the American Legion"; comparable comments have been made about other agencies. The national reclamation program was mainly developed by the Bureau of Reclamation with help and pressure from the National Reclamation Association. Conversely, professional administrators are often persons of expertise and prestige; hence they speak with some authority, and interest groups desire and cultivate their support just as the administrators need theirs.

In attempting to sell their programs to the legislature, administrators cultivate friendly relations with legislators and are often aided by interest groups affected. Lobbying by administrators is restricted by laws prohibiting the spending of agency funds to influence legislation. Nevertheless, members of Congress generally accept and respect the right of the heads of departments and bureaus and their "legislative liaison agents" to explain and defend their programs. At the same time, executive agencies are vulnerable if they attempt to drum up public support and may have their appropriation cut or be subjected to an investigation. Public employees often lobby for administrative programs through their own professional organizations.

In addition to working with administrators, interest groups cultivate the popularly elected executives. Their authority to recommend legislation and to veto it has much influence on legislative attitudes. Interest groups seek presidential or gubernatorial endorsements of their programs and try to influence appointments to agencies with which the as-

[12]Raymond A. Bauer, Ithiel de Sola Pool, and Louis Anthony Dexter, *American Business and Public Policy*, Atherton Press, Inc., New York, 1963, p. 324. See also Andrew M. Scott and Margaret A. Hunt, *Congress and Lobbies: Image and Reality*, University of North Carolina Press, Chapel Hill, 1966.

sociation is vitally concerned. Presidents and governors often find it necessary or advisable to consult influential group leaders on certain appointments.

Although personal friendships with elected executives, department heads, and civil servants are a major channel through which private associations can influence both program planning and day-to-day administration, there are formal relationships as well. There are thousands of advisory committees at the state and national levels composed of prominent laymen and representatives from the various parties-in-interest, which enjoy legal or quasi-legal status. They afford representatives an opportunity to present their viewpoints directly to administrators and help the latter to identify those forces that are favorable or unfavorable. Skillful administrators may use the committees to obtain help in the struggle with the legislature. From the standpoint of fair play, a question can be raised about who is entitled to representation on the advisory bodies. If one particular group having direct interest in an agency is denied membership on the advisory council, is it being denied access to the administrative process?

Interest groups may be charged with the responsibility for administering a program. Occupational licensing boards in the states are often composed in whole or in part of representatives of the interest being regulated and operate more or less as a guild system. In many states, numerous boards deal with a wide variety of problems, from athletics and dairy products to tuberculosis and forestry, for which interest groups are expected to furnish or to suggest personnel.

Other arrangements require less official status but significant representation of interests. Humane societies aid in enforcing leash laws, as wilderness societies act as guardians and watchdogs in public recreational areas. Veterans, labor, pension, and other groups conduct educational programs to inform their memberships of their rights and responsibilities under the law. The American system of "administrative pluralism" provides opportunities for many groups to achieve effective representation in government beyond that afforded through the legislature.

Appeals to the judiciary Pressure groups utilize every phase of the political process, including appeals to the courts. Recourse to the judiciary is likely to be used after defeat or dissatisfaction at the hands of the legislature and executive. Some groups find it quicker and less costly to present their cases before the administrators and legislators than before the courts. Nevertheless, the courts have the authority to make rulings materially affecting the distribution of power among private groups, and litigation often becomes an important tactic. Judicial determination comes through judicial review, the interpretation of statutes, executive orders, treaties, and the Constitution itself. Judges have considerable discretion in issuing injunctions, awarding damages, and in making property settlements.

The National Association for the Advancement of Colored People, through a special legal and defense fund, has used much of its resources to win a fuller recognition and observance of black rights in the courts, after it failed in the "political" branches of the government.

Organized groups may use strategies other than test cases and direct suits. They may file *amici curiae* ("friend of the court") briefs providing the court with legal arguments on the issue in conflict. This affords intervention before a decision is made and provides an opportunity to make momentary alliances with other groups to affect the decisions of the judges. Some groups have formed letter-writing campaigns to the courts and in rare cases send delegations to the courts—tactics that are seldom effective. The organized bar in many communities evaluates candidates for the bench and at times in reality becomes the nominating mechanism. From time to time, other groups attempt to influence or to veto certain persons under consideration for a judicial appointment. Women's and other affirmative-action interests have won numerous victories in the courts—but have also suffered some defeats.

Resources and resourcefulness   In summary, spokesmen for interest groups try to get to where decisions are made—to reach the locus of effective power. Servicemen's groups go to the Veterans Administration and to the House Veterans' Affairs Committee. Farm leaders work through certain bureaus of the Department of Agriculture and congressional agricultural committees. Tactics and methods must be flexible. At times it may be advantageous to operate in the open; more often than not, it is better to be circumspect and less visible in lobbying or in attempting to influence administrative agencies and political parties. Groups opposing change may be successful in getting bills bottled up in rules and standing committees. They must neutralize the pressures for change while avoiding criticism for being obstructive. Proponents of change try to operate through the multiple points of access. They may try litigation or to retire enemies and elect friends. In some states the initiative process has gained results after failure at all other power points. It is a case of never giving up; when a group *loses* in one arena, it may *win* in another.

A narrow theory of lobbying based upon the decision-making structure of government alone seldom explains political influence. The successes of civil rights causes are probably due as much (and probably more) to the black vote and support by diverse non-civil rights groups as to the militant lobbying effort of black organizations. The fervor and intensity with which its group conducts its political efforts, as well as the relative importance of its political goals, affect its influence. Characteristics of an organization such as wealth or access to money and credit, social status, prestige, and level of education, are likely assets, as are the personal charisma of its leaders, popularity, friendships, and identification with a dominant ethnic stock or religion. Control over communications media, jobs, and information also provides significant resources. Factors beyond the group itself may affect its activity and weight in the community. The political climate at a given time may be friendly to certain groups and hostile or indifferent to others. Influence is understood and explained only by taking into account a wide range of factors.

PROBLEMS OF PRESSURE
GROUPS

Functions of pressure groups In focusing attention on lobbying (often a pejorative term), the useful functions of organized groups are sometimes overlooked. Their leaders not only formulate programs on behalf of their members but also provide specialized information to those in public authority. In turn the leadership reports to the members of how governmental activities directly affect them. Organized interests exercise a protective and "watchdog" service for their constituents and, indirectly, for the general public. Much salutary criticism of public officials and programs emanates from the private sector.

Broadly speaking, pressure groups provide a form of social, functional, and political representation supplanting the imperfect geographic representation by legislators who cannot adequately appreciate all the myriad of interests comprising their districts. Lack of party government may mean that neither party will be capable of enacting a program cherished by an individual. In a very real sense a political group is symbolic, and its existence may give assurance that at least someone is trying to put certain concerns on the public agenda or, conversely, to keep out disliked government intervention. It becomes important to see that the leadership and policies of the "private governments" are truly reflective of the membership. A significant part of the recent protest movement was the effort to provide more democratic internal governance of organizations.

The management of group power Groups wishing change struggle to get proposed policies on the public agenda while their opponents struggle to keep them off the agenda or to modify and emasculate them to protect their own constituents.[13] In this process the "public interest" remains elusive. But adherents of a democratic theory assume that there is a general-interest solution to certain problems. The solution may or may not meet the approval of a well-organized minority. The problem is how to safeguard the values and legitimate functions of pressure groups and promote the public interest as well. This calls for adjustment, management, and control of group activity.

Natural accommodation Conflict in the United States takes place largely within the framework of the "business civilization." The great competitors are the organized social and economic interests. They are, for the most part, dedicated to what is called capitalism as a style of life. What is more, this style of life tends to prevail over other interests and styles. As we observed earlier, even nonbusiness organizations have something of an upper-class tendency in their leadership. Given this acceptance of a common ideology, can the free interplay of heterogeneous group interests protect the general society by making it difficult for any one

[13]On the policy process, see Greenwald, *Group Power*, and James E. Anderson, David W. Brody, and Charles Bullock III, *Public Policy and Politics in America*, Duxbury Press, North Scitaote, Mass., 1978.

group to prevail over the interests of others? There are "rules of the game" that groups are expected to observe, and violations may result in charges of "unfair." The multiple group memberships of many upper-class citizens confront them with conflicting loyalties and cross-pressures that help to ameliorate viewpoints.

Political action by one group tends to stimulate counteraction by others, with multiplication of groups helping to provide balance and restraint. J. K. Galbraith sees "countervailing" forces in the world of commerce and industry. Buyers or customers on one side of the market may combine and act as a check on producers and sellers on the other side. This looks good on paper, but there are numerous instances where no significant counterforce exists or can easily be built up, thus making it difficult for the principle to be realized. In fact it is hard to ascertain the extent to which countervailing forces now prevail or ever could prevail.

For example it is difficult to offset the "highway lobby" of truckers, contractors, and others, or the military-industrial complex, which tries to maximize the incomes of particular constituencies by continued high defense expenditures. These groups in turn charge, in the interest of economic health, the safety and security of the highways, and adequate national defense, that insufficient funds are being expended. Environmental groups were successful in sidetracking the building of supersonic airplanes but were unable to stop the Alaska pipeline. Consumers and subsets of buyers have not been very successful in defeating tariff and foreign policies which are often costly to them.

Public control   Although the nongovernmental forces modify the influence of private groups, legislatures do not always accept the results of competing pressures as the "public interest." Subpublic and rival groups often call for the intervening hand of public regulation. Madison wrote in *The Federalist* that "the regulation of these various and interfering interests forms the principal task of modern legislation." Despite the emphasis on laissez faire, the American government has followed Madison's views. Banks, railroads, and stock exchanges are but a few of the businesses placed under specific regulation. Many others had certain of their activities controlled by general laws, such as the Sherman Anti-Trust Act. The Taft-Hartley Act brought the internal operation of labor unions under some control, and corrupt-practices legislation attempts to prohibit direct contributions in political campaigns by unions and corporations. Although these piecemeal measures constitute no solution for the broader problems of pressure, they have resulted in bringing some activities of some groups under public scrutiny.

Most states have lobbying laws, and Congress enacted the Federal Regulation of Lobbying law in 1946 requiring lobbyists to register and to give such information as the names of their employers, the amount spent in lobbying, and legislative objectives.[14] The federal law is a mis-

---

[14]The *Congressional Quarterly* periodically analyzes and summarizes the data on the registered lobbyists. For 1979 registrations see *Weekly Report*, August 18, 1979, pp. 1720–1735. See also National Industrial Council, *Synopses of State Lobbying Laws*, Washington, D.C., 1974.

nomer as there is virtually no regulation of lobbyists. Parts of the law are unclear, and the data regarding legislative objectives and expenditures are fragmentary. Lobby laws provide some information about lobbyists but do not control them and show little promise as balancers of interests.

The elected executives, civil servants, lawmakers, and judges have a sense of the public interest, and in diverse ways, within their constitutional authority, endeavor to manage and to ameliorate group demands. This is necessary for political survival. As representatives of broader constituencies than legislators, governors and Presidents are required to assume more and more responsibility for drafting policies and compromises that sift through private requests in an effort to promote the best interests of the commonweal. This should not obscure the fact that what we see is an expression of the principle of concurrent majorities. The function of formal government is often one of legitimatizing decisions hammered out in conferences among interested groups. The legislature is seen as delaying endorsement of a proposal evolved by the free play of groups until these groups have reached some agreement. But government as a central decision maker may intervene to see that "public values" are achieved or at least not ignored. It may impose some restraints and controls and help the private interests find an optimal position. But government intervention also has a positive side of assisting the underprivileged and unorganized groups and setting a tone of fair play. The decentralized system of arriving at public decisions is complicated, and if its results are to be satisfactory, there must be understanding and tolerance and a sense of responsibility on the part of interest-group leadership as well as of those in public authority. Government is the prime agent for providing unity in the midst of diversity.

The new politics   An increase in the tempo and intensity of pressure-group activity is manifesting itself with a different emphasis, if not in new ways. Many of the traditional ways of protesting and of controlling protest are ineffective. Public laws forbidding civil servants and public employees from striking have been honored in the breach by postal workers, teachers, sanitation employees, air traffic controllers, and bus drivers among others. Despite "illegal" stoppages, many employees won substantial concessions and benefits from the tactics. As blacks, the poor, students, and antiwar protestors have resorted to sit-ins and "taking to the streets" tactics, authorities have often found it necessary to employ police and to make changes in order to restore order. Dissidents seek ways of refining techniques to maximize their effectiveness. In turn, authorities seek new ways to manage the conflicts. A major task of today is to control disruption without eradicating popular participation.

Population increases and vast technological changes have given rise to more and newer aspirations leading to new citizens' organizations, which some older organizations see as a threat. The more militant organizations are particular subjects of controversy and cause problems of accommodation and negotiation often ending in placing issues before the courts.

In a broad sort of way, the new politics is becoming a search for new political devices and mechanisms, much as the Progressives, in the earlier part of the century, developed party primaries, popular lawmaking, direct election of senators, and women's suffrage to bring about more effective control of government through popular participation. The new politics of today has resulted in placing representatives of specific minorities and those previously unrepresented on decision-making boards. Proportional representation is seeing some revival as a method of electing school and other councils. The concept of "decentralization," with local areas making their own decisions, is attractive in principal to local leaders who are without power, and is often embraced by them as the "new politics." There is also a demand for new agencies and mechanisms to bring about a greater degree of "participatory democracy" such as citizen planning boards, civilian review boards, or an ombudsman. The political society is now facing the question of the degree to which incremental changes in existing institutions and procedures will satisfy politicized groups, and where entirely new institutions and approaches are necessary if public disorder is to be avoided and the good things in life made be available to all in the society.

The American pluralist democracy of interest-group politics reflecting competing interests has come under increasing criticism in terms of its adequacy to meet the great economic and political problems now facing the United States.[15] It is argued that natural accommodation with countervailing forces, aggregation of interests by the political parties, and elections have in themselves been insufficient in controlling the swirl of pluralistic interests. Congress reflects the decentralization of the political system as a whole. Recent Presidents, while in the position of being best able to view the interests of the national constituency, were often limited in their powers and in their ability to get action from Congress. Even so, the President is in a position to symbolize and often act in helping to fulfill the aspirations of those who are unable to attain their goals in a laissez faire system. The 1980s must continue the search for a more efficacious functioning of American pluralism.

REVIEW QUESTIONS

1 What political interests do you have? Are these satisfactorily represented by your legislator and by the interest groups to which you belong?

2 What are the most influential pressure groups in your state? What criteria did you use in evaluating this political strength? Would you have arrived at a different conclusion if you had used different criteria? What are some of the less effectual pressure groups in your state? Why are they ineffective?

3 What is the "countervailing" theory of pressure politics? Give examples where this principle appears to operate in your area. With which

[15]One of the more widely read critiques is that of Theodore J. Lowi, *The End of Liberalism: Ideology, Policy, and the Crises of Public Authority*, W. W. Norton & Company, New York, 1969.

particular groups does it not seem to work? Do these groups need controls? Why or why not?

4 Evaluate the principal tactics that interest groups use to achieve their goals.

5 Is the "public interest" the resultant of the clashing of groups interests?

6 Does the pluralistic society, the society of diversity, have any weaknesses? Cound they be remedied by forces for unity without endangering the values of diversity?

7 Can the use of force and violence as protest by private persons and groups be justified in any case? Why or why not?

FOR FURTHER READING

Adamany, David W., and George E. Agree: *Political Money*, Johns Hopkins University Press, Baltimore, 1975.

Agranoff, Robert: *The Management of Election Campaigns*, Holbrook Press, Boston, 1976.

Alexander, Herbert E.: *Money in Politics*, Public Affairs Press, Washington, D.C., 1972.

_____ (ed.): *Campaign Money: Reform and Reality in the States*, The Free Press, New York, 1976.

Banfield, Edward C.: *Political Influence*, The Free Press, New York, 1961.

Barber, James D. (ed.): *Race for the Presidency: The Media and the Nominating Process*, American Assembly, Columbia University, Prentice-Hall, Englewood Cliffs, N.J., 1978.

Baskin, Daryl: *American Pluralist Democracy: A Critique*, Van Nostrand Reinhold Company, New York, 1971.

Berelson, Bernard, Paul F. Lazarsfeld, and William N. McPhee: *Voting*, The University of Chicago Press, Chicago, 1954.

Binkley, Wilfred E.: *American Political Parties: Their Natural History*, 4th ed., Alfred A. Knopf, Inc., New York, 1963.

Bone, Hugh A.: *American Politics and the Party System*, 4th ed., McGraw-Hill Book Company, New York, 1971.

_____: *Party Committees and National Politics*, University of Washington Press, Seattle, Wash., 1958.

_____: *Political Party Management*, General Learning Corporation, Morristown, N.J., 1973.

Burnham, Walter Dean: *Critical Elections and the Mainsprings of American Politics*, W. W. Norton & Company, Inc., New York, 1970.

Campbell, Angus, Philip E. Converse, Warren E. Miller, and Donald E. Stokes: *The American Voter*, John Wiley & Sons, Inc., New York, 1960.

_____, _____, _____, and _____: *Elections and the Political Order*, John Wiley & Sons, Inc., New York, 1966.

_____, Gerald Gurin, and Warren E. Miller: *The Voter Decides*, Harper & Row, Publishers, Inc., New York, 1954.

Campbell, Bruce A.: *The American Electorate*, Holt, Rinehart, and Winston, New York, 1979.

Chambers, William C., and Walter Dean Burnham (eds.): *The American Party Systems: Stages of Political Development*, Oxford University Press, New York, 1967.

Congressional Quarterly: *The Washington Lobby*, Washington, D.C., 1979.

Crotty, William J.: *Decision for the Democrats: Reforming the Party Structure*, Johns Hopkins University Press, Baltimore, 1978.

Dahl, Robert A.: *Who Governs?*, Yale University Press, New Haven, Conn., 1961.

David, Paul T., Ralph M. Goldman, and Richard C. Bain: *The Politics of National Party Conventions*, The Brookings Institution, Washington, D.C., 1960.

Dawson, Richard E., and Kenneth Prewitt: *Political Socialization*, Little, Brown and Company, Boston, 1969.

Eldersveld, Samuel J.: *Political Parties: A Behavioral Analysis*, Rand McNally & Company, Chicago, 1964.

Fishel, Jeff: *Party and Opposition: Congressional Challenges in American Politics*, David McKay Company, Inc., New York, 1973.

————— (ed.): *Parties and Elections in an Anti-Party Age*, Indiana University Press, Bloomington, Ind., 1978.

Greenwald, Carol S.: *Group Power: Lobbying and Public Policy*, Praeger Publications, 1977.

Hadley, Arthur T.: *The Empty Polling Booth*, Prentice-Hall, Inc., Englewood Cliffs, N.J., 1978.

Heard, Alexander: *The Costs of Democracy*, The University of North Carolina Press, Chapel Hill, N.C., 1960.

Herring, Pendleton: *The Politics of Democracy: American Politics in Action*, W. W. Norton & Company, Inc., New York, 1965.

Holtzman, Abraham: *Interest Groups and Lobbying*, The Macmillan Company, New York, 1966.

Hyman, Herbert H.: *Political Socialization*, The Free Press, New York, 1959.

Jacob, Herbert, and Kenneth N. Vines (eds.): *Politics in the American States: A Comparative Analysis*, 3d ed., Little, Brown and Company, Boston, 1976.

James, Judson L.: *American Political Parties*, Pegasus, New York, 1969.

Jewell, Malcolm, and David M. Olson: *American State Political Parties and Elections*, The Dorsey Press, Homewood, Ill., 1978.

Keech, William R., and Donald R. Matthews: *The Party's Choice*, The Brookings Institution, Washington, D.C., 1976.

Key, V. O., Jr.: *The Responsible Electorate*, The Belknap Press, Harvard University Press, Cambridge, Mass., 1966.

King, Anthony (ed.): *The New American Political System*, American Enterprise Institute for Public Policy Research, Washington, D.C., 1978.

Kirkpatrick, Jeane J.: *The New Presidential Elite*, Russell Sage Foundation and Twentieth Century Fund, New York, 1976.

Klapper, Joseph T.: *The Effects of Mass Communication*, The Free Press, New York, 1960.

Kleppner, Paul: *The Third Electoral System, 1853-1892: Parties, Votes, and Political*, University of North Carolina Press, Chapel Hill, N.C., 1979.

Kraus, Sidney, and Dennis Davis: *The Effects of Mass Communication* on *Political Behavior*, Pennsylvania State University Press, University Park, Pa., 1978.

Ladd, Everett Carll, Jr.: *American Political Parties*, W. W. Norton & Company, 1970.

_____: *Transformations of the American Party System: Political Coalitions from the New Deal to the 1970s*, W. W. Norton & Company, New York, 1978.

Lazarsfeld, Paul F., Bernard R. Berelson, and Hazel Gaudet: *The People's Choice*, 2d ed., Columbia University Press, New York, 1948.

Leiserson, Avery: *Parties and Politics*, Alfred A. Knopf, Inc., New York, 1958.

Lipset, Seymour Martin: *Political Man*, Doubleday & Company, Inc., Garden City, N.Y., 1960.

Lowi, Theodore J.: *The End of Liberalism: Ideology, Policy and the Crisis of Public Authority*, W. W. Norton & Company, Inc., New York, 1969.

Malbin, Michael J. (ed.): *Parties, Interest Groups and Campaign Finance Laws*, American Enterprise Institute for Public Policy Research. Washington, D.C., 1980.

Merriam, Charles E., and Harold F. Gosnell: *Non-Voting*, The University of Chicago Press, Chicago, 1924.

Milbrath, Lester W.: *Political Participation*, Rand McNally & Company, Chicago, 1965.

Miller, Warren E., and Teresa F. Levitin: *Leadership and Change: The New Politics and the American Electorate*, Winthrop Publishers, Cambridge, Mass., 1976.

Naider, Donald H.: *When Governments Come to Washington: Governors, Mayors, and Intergovernmental Lobbying*, The Free Press, New York, 1974.

Nie, Norman H., Sidney Verba, and John R. Petrocik: *The Changing American Voter*, Harvard University Press, Cambridge, Mass., 1976.

Parris, Judith H.: *The Convention Problem: Issues in Reform of Presidential Nominating Procedures*, The Brookings Institution, Washington, D.C., 1972.

Peirce, Neil R.: *The People's President: The Electoral College in American History and Direct-Vote Alternative*, Simon and Schuster, Inc., New York, 1968.

Polsby, Nelson W., and Aaron Wildavsky: *Presidential Elections*, Charles Scribner's Sons, New York, 1976.

Pomper, Gerald M.: *Elections in America*, Dodd, Mead & Company, Inc., New York, 1968.

_____: *Voters' Choice: Varieties of Electoral Behavior*, Dodd, Mead & Company, New York, 1975.

Ranney, Austin: *Curing the Mischiefs of Faction: Party Reform in America*, University of California Press, Berkeley, Calif., 1975.

_____ and Willmoore Kendall, *Democracy and the American Party System*, Harcourt, Brace & Company, New York, 1956.

Reis, John C.: *Public Financing of Political Campaigns: Reform or Ripoff?*, Institute of Government and Public Affairs, University of California, Los Angeles, 1974.

Saffell, David C.: *Watergate: Its Effects on the American Political System*, Winthrop Publishers, Inc., Cambridge, Mass., 1974.

Scott, Ruth K.: *Parties in Crisis: Party Politics in America*, John Wiley & Sons, New York, 1979.

Sorauf, Frank J.: *Party Politics in America*, Little, Brown and Company, Boston, 1972.

Wiebe, Robert H.: *The Segmented Society: An Introduction to the Meaning of America*, Oxford University Press, New York, 1975.

Young, James P.: *The Politics of Affluence: Ideology in the United States Since World War II*, Chandler Publishing Company, San Francisco, 1968.

INDEX

Activists, 2, 57 – 58, 67
  educational level of, 119
  in pressure groups, 101 – 108
  (*See also* Opinion leaders)
Adamany, David W., 92*n.*
Administrative agencies, lobbying
  of, 116 – 117
Adrian, Charles, 68*n.*
AFL-CIO (American Federation of
  Labor-Congress of Industrial
  Organizations), 89, 104
AFL-CIO Committee for Political
  Education, 89, 112
Age:
  as requirement for voting, 4 – 5
  and voting turnout, 17 – 18
Agnew, Spiro, 82, 83, 88, 92
Agranoff, Robert, 86*n.*
Agree, George E., 92*n.*
Agricultural groups, 105 – 106
Agriculture, U.S. Department of, 105,
  118
Alexander, Herbert E., 92*n.*
American Bankers Association, 104
American Bar Association, 100
American Farm Bureau Federation,
  21, 105 – 106
American Federation of Musicians,
  100
American Federation of Teachers,
  106
American Israel Public Affairs
  Committee, 108
American Legion, 107, 116
American Medical Association
  (AMA), 21, 100, 107
American Medical Association
  Political Action Committee, 94

American Petroleum Institute, 104
American Veterans Committee, 107
American voters compared with
  democratic ideal, 40 – 44
Americans for Democratic Action,
  89
Apoliticals, 2 – 3

Bachrach, Peter, 43*n.*
Baker, Howard, 82
Ballot propositions, 47, 113
Barker, James D., 78*n.*
Bauer, Raymond A., 116
Berelson, Bernard R., 11*n.*, 17*n.*,
  25*n.*, 37*n.*, 38
Binkley, W. E., 50*n.*
Bishop, George F., 92*n.*
Black Muslims, 107
Blacks:
  as involuntary nonvoters, 5
  as pressure groups, 48, 107 – 108,
    111
  voting restrictions on, 35
Bone, Hugh A., 55*n.*
Brodbeck, Arthur J., 41*n.*
Brody, David W., 119*n.*
Brody, Richard A., 13*n.*, 14*n.*
Brown, Jerry, 78, 81, 95
Brown, Thad A., 9*n.*
Buckley v. Valeo, 94
Bullock, Charles, III, 119*n.*
Burdick, Eugene, 41*n.*
Bureau of Reclamation, 116
Burke, Edmund, 49
Burns, James M., 63*n.*
Business groups, 103 – 104
Butler, David, 1*n.*

California Democratic Council, 75
California Republican Assembly, 75
California Walnut Growers
Association, 105
Campaigns, 85 – 96
funds for, 2, 59, 92 – 95
methods for, 90 – 92
mass media, 56, 78, 79, 90 – 92
organization of, 88 – 90
publicity for, 69
strategy in, 85 – 88
uses of, 95 – 96
Campbell, Angus, 6*n*., 13*n*., 17*n*.,
34*n*. – 37*n*., 40*n*.
Campbell, Bruce A., 2*n*., 25*n*.
Canadian political parties, 53 – 54
Candidates:
orientation of, 9, 11, 84 – 85
and pressure groups, 111 – 113
Carter, Jimmy, 8, 9, 11, 14, 27, 28, 40,
41, 52, 55, 62, 72, 78, 81 – 83,
87, 88, 95
Categoric groups, 15 – 19
by age, 17 – 18
defined, 15
by education, 19
by sex, 17
Caucus, party, 73
Celler, Emanuel, 113
Center for Political Studies,
University of Michigan
(formerly Survey Research
Center), 6*n*., 8, 18, 19, 37, 40
Chamber of Commerce of the United
States, 104, 106
Church, Ralph, 78, 81
Citizen, ideal, compared to
American voting practices,
42 – 44
Citizenship requirement for voting, 4
Cognitive maps, voters', 10 – 14
conceptualization in, 12 – 13
defined, 10
perception in, 11 – 12
political involvement in, 13 – 14
Committee to Re-elect the President
(Nixon administration), 90
Common Cause (organization), 108

Communications, 26 – 29
interpersonal, 28 – 29
leaders of, 28 – 29
mass, 26 – 28
(*See also* Mass media)
Conceptualization of political reality,
12 – 13
Confrontations used by pressure
groups, 110
Congress:
nominations for, 76 – 77
Republican party in, 61 – 62
Congressional parties, 60 – 61,
63 – 64
Connally, John, 87
Consumer groups, 109
Contributions, campaign, 2, 59,
92 – 95
Conventions (*see* National
conventions)
Converse, Philip, 6*n*., 10*n*., 13*n*.,
17*n*., 19*n*., 21*n*., 24*n*., 26*n*.,
34*n*. – 38*n*.
Cotter, Cornelius P., 58*n*.
Courts (*see* Judiciary)
Cross-pressured voters, 9 – 10, 26,
35

Dahl, Robert A., 43*n*.
Davis, Dennis, 27*n*.
Debates on television, 27 – 28,
91 – 92
Delegates for national conventions,
78 – 79
Democratic Advisory Council, 59
Democratic ideal, voters
compared with, 40 – 44
Democratic party:
Advisory Council, 59
attitudes toward, 20 – 22, 38
in Congress, 60 – 61
development of, 50 – 52
1972 convention, 79 – 81
1974 convention, 61
Democratic Steering and Policy
Committee, 60
Democratic Study Group (DSG), 60

Demonstrations used by pressure groups, 110
Dennis, Jack, 7*n*.
Department of Agriculture, U.S., 105, 118
Deviating elections, 35 − 36
De Vries, Walter, 40*n*.
Dewey, Thomas E., 11, 81
Dexter, Louis A., 116*n*.
Direct primaries (*see* Elections, primary)
Docking, Robert, 40
Dole, Robert, 82

Eagleton, Thomas, 82, 83
Easton, David, 6*n*.
Edison Electric Institute, 104
Education:
  and pressure groups, 106
  role in voting behavior, 19
Eisenhower, Dwight D., 9, 12, 38, 55, 78, 81, 83, 88
Elder, Shirley, 114*n*.
Elections:
  deviating, 35 − 36
  frequency of, 3 − 4
  local, 37 − 39
    national loyalties in, 39
  maintaining, 35 − 36
  nonpartisan, 39, 67 − 69, 89, 112 − 113
  preprimary conventions, 75
  and pressure groups, 112 − 113
  primary, 32 − 33, 73 − 77
  realigning, 35 − 36
  regulation of, 3 − 5, 34
  and social groups (*see* Social groups)
  state and local, 39
  ticket splitting in, 39 − 40, 55, 70
  turnout for (*see* Voting turnout)
  (*See also* Campaigns; Nominations; *entries beginning with terms:* Voter; Voting)
Elites, 1, 101 − 103
Environmental groups, 108

Epstein, Leon, 33*n*.
Ethnic groups, 23 − 24, 107 − 108
  (*See also* Minorities)
Executive parties, 61 − 63

Family influences on voting, 24 − 25
Farmers' Union, 105
Federal corrupt practices legislation, 93 − 95
Federal Election Commission, 93, 94
Federal Regulation of Lobbying law, 120 − 121
Federalist party, 50 − 51
Ford, Gerald, 8, 11, 14, 27 − 28, 41, 62, 79, 82 − 83, 88, 95
Funds, campaign, 2, 59, 92 − 95

Galbraith, J. K., 120*n*.
Garson, G. David., 103*n*.
Gaudet, Hazel, 17*n*.
Goldwater, Barry, 9, 29, 59*n*., 70, 81 − 83, 87
Gosnell, Harold F., 17*n*.
Government:
  "open," 71 − 72, 108
  political parties in, 60 − 64
  voter impact on, 40 − 45
  [*See also* Congress; Judiciary; Legislature(s); President]
Greenstein, Fred I., 7*n*.
Greenwald, Gerald, 24*n*.
Gurin, Gerald, 24*n*.

Hadley, Arthur T., 35*n*.
Halleck, Charles, 82
Hamilton, Alexander, 50
Harris, Louis, 7*n*.
Harris, Richard, 115*n*.
Hayakawa, S. I., 92
Helms, Jesse, 92
Hennessy, Bernard C., 58*n*.
Hess, Robert, 7*n*.
Hesseltine, W. B., 65*n*.
Hoover, Herbert, 67

Hrebenar, Ronald J., 80*n.*
Humphrey, Hubert, 10, 78, 81, 83
Hunt, Margaret A., 116*n.*
Hyman, Herbert H., 17*n.*

Independents, 6, 8
Interest groups (*see* Pressure groups)
Interpersonal communications, 28–29
Inter-University Consortium for Political Research, 10*n.*
Issue orientation, 8–10
Issues in campaigns, 85, 86

Jackson, Andrew, 52, 90
Jackson, Henry, 52
Jackson-Beeck, Marilyn, 92*n.*
Jefferson, Thomas, 42, 50, 52
Jewell, Malcolm, 55*n.*
Johnson, Lyndon B., 42, 55, 87
Jones, Charles D., 60*n.*
Judge, Thomas, 40
Judiciary:
    Buckley v. Valeo, 94
    lobbying in, 117–118
    role in "new politics," 121

Karp, Walter, 59*n.*
Katz, Elihu, 28*n.*, 29*n.*
Kelly, Stanley, Jr., 96*n.*
Kendall, Willmoore, 43*n.*
Kennedy, John F., 20, 27*n.*, 28*n.*, 52, 78, 82, 88, 91
Key, V. O., Jr., 36*n.*, 39
King, Anthony, 14*n.*, 21*n.*
Kirkpatrick, Jeane J., 17*n.*, 21*n.*
Kissinger, Henry, 88
Klapper, Paul T., 27*n.*
Knights of Labor, 104
Kramer, Michael S., 24*n.*
Kraus, Sidney, 27*n.*, 29*n.*

Labor groups, 104–105, 112
Ladd, Everett Carll, Jr., 50*n.*

La Follette, Robert M., 64
Landon, Alfred, 81
Lazarsfeld, Paul F., 11*n.*, 17*n.*, 25*n.*, 28*n.*, 37*n.*, 38*n.*
Leadership:
    opinion leaders, 2, 28–29
        in pressure groups, 102–105
    of political parties, 65–67
League of Women Voters, 100
Lee, Eugene, 68*n.*
Legal restrictions on voting, 4–5
Legislature(s):
    citizen bypass of, 47
    lobbying in, 113–117
Levy, Mark R., 24*n.*
Lincoln, Abraham, 52
Literacy test, 5
Lobbying:
    in administrative agencies, 116–117
    in judiciary, 117–118
    in legislature, 113–117
    (*See also* Pressure groups)
Local elections, 37–39
    national loyalties in, 39
Locke, John, 42
Lowi, Theodore, Jr., 102*n.*

McCarthy, Eugene, 87
McClure, Robert, 27*n.*
McGovern, George, 9–10, 40, 43, 52, 59*n.*, 70*n.*, 81–84, 87, 88, 91, 92
Mackenzie, W. J. M., 1*n.*
McPhee, William N., 25*n.*, 37*n.*
Madison, James, 98–120
Maintaining elections, 35–36
Mass media:
    in campaigns, 56, 78, 79, 90–92
        television debates, 27–28, 91–92
    effect on voting behavior, 28
    in nominations, 78
    political content of, 26–28
    use by pressure groups, 109–110
Matthews, Donald R., 77*n.*, 81
Mazmanian, Daniel A., 65*n.*
Meadow, Robert G., 65*n.*

Media (*see* Mass media)
Merriam, Charles E., 17*n.*
Metropolitan areas, voter
    preferences in, 37 – 38
Milbrath, Lester W., 2*n.*
Miller, Arthur H., 9*n.*
Miller, Warren E., 6*n.*, 9*n.*, 10*n.*, 13*n.*,
    17*n.*, 24*n.*, 26*n.*, 34*n.* – 36*n.*,
    40*n.*
Minor parties, 54, 64 – 65, 111
Minorities:
  ethnic and religious, as pressure
    groups, 48, 107 – 108
  in national conventions, 79 – 80
  political activity of, 23 – 24, 48, 111
  (*See also* Blacks; Women; *specific
    minority organization*)
Mondale, Walter, 83
Money in elections, 2, 59, 92 – 95
Motivation and nonvoting, 35
Muskie, Edmund, 81, 88

Nader, Ralph, 109
National Association for the
    Advancement of Colored
    People (NAACP), 16, 107,
    117 – 118
National Association of
    Broadcasters, 103
National Association of
    Manufacturers, 104
National Beef Growers Association,
    105
National Catholic Welfare
    Conference, 108
National committees, 57 – 58
National conventions, 77 – 85
  composition of, 79 – 80
  criticism of, 83 – 85
  preconvention maneuvers for,
    77 – 79
  rules adopted in, 80 – 81
  selection of delegates for, 78 – 79
National Council of Churches of
    Christ, 108
National Education Association, 21,
    106
National Grange, 105

National Reclamation Association,
    116
National Retail Dry Goods
    Association, 103
National Rifle Association, 115
National Urban League, 107
"New politics," 121 – 122
Nie, Norman H., 40*n.*
Nimmo, Dan, 86*n.*
Nixon, Richard, 10, 27, 28, 39, 40, 43,
    62, 71, 81, 83, 88, 91, 92
Nominations:
  by caucus, 73
  for Congress, 76 – 77
  by national convention (*see*
    National conventions)
  for President, 77 – 82
  by primary, 73 – 76
  by state convention, 73
  for Vice President, 82 – 83
Nonpartisan politics, 39, 67 – 69, 89,
    112 – 113
Nonvoting, 2, 5, 6, 35
  (*See also* Voting turnout)

Occupational groups, 21
Olson, David M., 55*n.*
Olson, Marcus, Jr., 100
"Open" government, 71 – 72, 108
Opinion leaders, 2, 28 – 29
  in pressure groups, 102 – 105
Organization activists (*see* Activists)
Ornstein, Norman, Jr., 114*n.*

Parsons, Talcott, 41*n.*
Participatory democracy, 42 – 44
Parties (*see* Political parties)
Party caucus, 73
Party government, theory of, 63 – 64
Party identification, 6 – 8
  in campaign strategy, 89
  influenced by social
    desegregation, 37
  and interest in politics, 14
  by regions, 36 – 37
Patronage, 52
Patterson, Thomas E., 27*n.*

Peabody, Robert L., 60*n*.
Peck, G. Wayne, 114*n*.
Peer group influence on voting behavior, 25 – 26
Penniman, Howard R., 1*n*.
People United to Save Humanity (PUSH), 107
Perception of political reality, 11 – 12
Personality:
    of candidates, 9, 11, 84 – 85
    and leadership, 66 – 67
Petrosik, John R., 40*n*.
Platforms, party, 59, 80
Pluralism, 44, 48, 92, 99, 122
Pluralists vs. elitists, 103
Political-action committees (PACs), 94, 111
Political campaigns (*see* Campaigns)
Political involvement as aspect of voters' cognitive maps, 13 – 14
Political parties:
    contributors, 2, 94
    criticism of, 69, 71
    defined, 49
    development of, 50 – 52
    finances of, 59
    in government, 60 – 64
    leadership of, 65 – 67
    minor, 54, 64 – 65, 111
    money in elections, 2, 59, 92 – 95
    organization of, 56 – 59
    platforms, 59, 80
    recruitment function of, 56 – 59
    relation to pressure groups, 110 – 113
    state, 54 – 56
    under stress, 69 – 72
    variations on two-party system, 54 – 56
    (*See also* Democratic party; Party identification; Republican party; Third parties; Two-party system)
Polls, public opinion, 69, 79, 87
Polsby, Nelson B., 86*n*.
Pomper, Gerald, 96*n*., 112*n*.

Pool, Ithiel de Sola, 116
President:
    nomination of, 77 – 82
    as party leader, 61 – 63
Pressure groups:
    and administrators, 116 – 117
    and candidates, 111 – 113
    control of, 119 – 121
    and courts, 117 – 118
    defined, 99 – 100
    electoral activity of, 112 – 113
    ethnic and religious minorities as, 48, 107 – 108
    leadership of, 101 – 103
    lobbying by (*see* Lobbying)
    major, 103 – 107
    membership of, 100 – 103
        (*See also specific organizations*)
    and the "new politics," 121 – 122
    public-interest and single-issue organizations as, 70, 108 – 109
    and public policy, 46 – 48, 113 – 118
    public relations of, 109 – 110
    reasons for, 98 – 100
    relations with parties, 110 – 113
Primary elections, 32 – 33, 73 – 77
Primary groups, 16, 24 – 25
Professional groups, 106 – 107
Proposition 13 (California), 47, 113
Protest movements, 64 – 65
Public-interest groups, 108 – 109
Public opinion polls, 79, 87
Public policy:
    decentralization and, 46 – 47
    pressure-group influences on, 47 – 48, 113 – 118
Public relations of pressure groups, 109 – 110

Qualifications, legal, for voting, 4 – 5

Railroad Brotherhoods, 104
Raine, Alden S., 9*n*.
Rampton, Calvin, 40

Ranney, Austin, 28*n.*, 32*n.*, 33*n.*, 43*n.*, 47*n.*, 63*n.*, 77*n.*
Reagan, Ronald, 78, 81−83, 95
Realigning elections, 35−36
Reference groups, 15−16, 102
(*See also* Social groups)
Registration, voter, 4−5, 34
Religion and voting behavior, 20
Religious groups, 20, 108
Republican party:
    attitudes toward, 7, 20−22
    in Congress, 61−62
    development of, 50−52
Republican Policy Committee, 59−60
Residence requirements, 4
Ripley, Randall, 60*n.*
Roosevelt, Franklin D., 52, 81−82
Roosevelt, Theodore, 52−53
Rosenstone, Steven J., 5*n.*, 34*n.*
Rousseau, Jean-Jacques, 42
Rural areas, voter preferences in, 37, 38
Rusk, Jerrold G., 10*n.*

Salmon, Thomas, 40
Savage, Robert L., 86*n.*
Scammon, Richard M., 32*n.*
Schattschneider, E. E., 100*n.*
Schlesinger, Joseph A., 54
Schumpeter, Joseph, 43*n.*
Schweiker, Richard, 82
Scott, Andrew, 116*n.*
Scott, Ruth R., 80*n.*
Secondary groups, 16, 20−24
    defined, 18
    ethnic, 23−24, 48, 107−108
    influences on voting behavior, 20−21
    occupational, 21
    social class, 21−23, 34
Sectionalism, 36−37
Sexual differences in political preferences, 17
(*See also* Women)
Sherrill, Robert, 115*n.*
Shriver, Sargent, 82, 92

Sierra Club, 108
Single-issue politics, 70, 108−109
Sniderman, Paul M., 13*n.*
Social class, effect on voting, 21−23, 34
Social groups:
    categoric groups (*see* Categoric groups)
    primary groups, 16, 24−25
    secondary groups (*see* Secondary groups)
Socialists, 64
Socioeconomic status, role in voting, 21−23, 34
Soul City (organization), 107
Southern Christian Leadership Conference, 107
Special-interest contributions, 2, 94
Split-ticket voting, 39−40, 55, 70
Stalin, Joseph, 49
State committees, 57−58
State conventions, 73
State and local elections, 39
State political parties, 54−56
Stevenson, Adlai, 78, 82, 89−90
Stokes, Donald E., 6*n.*, 13*n.*, 17*n.*, 25*n.*, 34*n.*−38*n.*
Strategy in campaigns, 85−88
Suburbs, voter preferences in, 37−38
Suffrage, 3−5
Sullivan, Henry Stack, 11
Survey Research Center (*see* Center for Political Studies)

Taft-Hartley Act, 8, 120
Tarrance, V. Lance, 40*n.*
Teamsters, 104
Television (*see* Mass media)
Television debates, 27−28, 91−92
Third parties, 54, 64−66, 111
Ticket splitting, 39−40, 55, 70
Tocqueville, Alexis de, 98, 107
Trade associations, 103−104
Tribbitt, Sherman, 40
Truman, Harry S, 11, 23
Turnout, voting (*see* Voting turnout)

Two-party system:
  effect on voters, 41
  reasons for, 53
  variations on, 54−56

Udall, Morris, 78, 81
United Auto Workers, 21, 114
United States Brewers Association, 104
U.S. Department of Agriculture, 105, 118
Urban areas, voter preferences in, 37−38

Variables in voting behavior, 5−10
Verba, Sidney, 40*n.*
Veterans Administration, 116, 118
Veterans of Foreign Wars (VFW), 107
Veterans' groups, 107
Vice President, nomination of, 82−83
Violence as political technique, 110
Voter impact on government, 40−45
Voter registration, 4−5, 34
Voters' cognitive maps (*see* Cognitive maps, voters')
Voters compared with democratic ideal, 40−44

Voting qualifications, 4−5
Voting Rights Act of 1965, 3−5
Voting turnout, 13, 17−18, 31−35
  nonvoting, 2, 5, 6, 35
  (*See also* Elections)

Walker, Jack L., 43*n.*
Wallace, George, 59*n.*, 65, 87
Washington, George, 49
Watergate affair, 44, 69, 90
Wattenberg, Ben J., 7*n.*
Whig party, 50−51, 54
White, Theodore H., 86*n.*
Wildavsky, Aaron, 86*n.*
Willkie, Wendell, 78, 81, 83
Wilson, James Q., 99*n.*
Wilson, Woodrow, 52
Wolfe, Arthur C., 10*n.*
Wolfinger, Raymond E., 5*n.*, 34*n.*
Women:
  in national conventions, 79−80
  political behavior as group, 17

Young, Andrew, 108

Zeigler, Harmon, 99*n.*